THE TEN-MINUTE PRINCIPAL

With love for my wife, Cookie, who supported and encouraged me throughout the writing of this book.

—Evan Robb

THE **TEN-MINUTE** PRINCIPAL

Free Up Your Time to Focus on Leadership

EVAN ROBB

FOR INFORMATION:

Corwin

A SAGE Company

2455 Teller Road

Thousand Oaks, California 91320

www.corwin.com

SAGE Ltd.

1 Oliver's Yard

55 City Road

London, EC1Y 1SP

United Kingdom

SAGE Pvt. Ltd.

B 1/I 1 Mohan Cooperative Industrial Area

Mathura Road, New Delhi 110 044

India

SAGE Publications Asia-Pacific Pte. Ltd.

18 Cross Street #10–10/11/12

China Square Central

Singapore 048423

Publisher: Arnis Burvikovs

Development Editor: Desirée A. Bartlett

Senior Editorial Assistant: Eliza B. Erickson

Marketing Manager: Sharon Pendergast

Production Editor: Veronica Stapleton Hooper

Copy Editor: Amy Hanquist Harris

Typesetter: Hurix Digital

Proofreader: Barbara Coster

Indexer: Beth Nauman-Montana

Cover Designer: Alexa Turner

Interior Designer: Janet Kiesel

Printed in the United States of America

Library of Congress Cataloging-in-Publication Data
Names: Robb, Evan, author.

Title: The ten-minute principal : free up your time to focus on leadership / Evan Robb.

Description: First edition. | Thousand Oaks, California : Corwin, 2019. | Includes bibliographical references and index.

Identifiers: LCCN 2018061726 | ISBN 9781544345574 (pbk. : alk. paper)

Subjects: LCSH: School principals—United States—Handbooks, manuals, etc. | School management and organization--United States—Handbooks, manuals, etc. | Educational leadership—United States—Handbooks, manuals, etc.

Classification: LCC LB2831.92 .R626 2019 | DDC 371.2/012—dc23 LC record available at https://lccn.loc.gov/2018061726

This book is printed on acid-free paper.

Certified Chain of Custody
SUSTAINABLE FORESTRY INITIATIVE
Promoting Sustainable Forestry
www.sfiprogram.org
SFI-01268

SFI label applies to text stock

19 20 21 22 23 10 9 8 7 6 5 4 3 2 1

CONTENTS

Note from the Publisher: The author has provided video and web content throughout the book that are available to you through QR (quick response) codes. To read a QR code, you must have a smartphone or tablet with a camera. We recommend that you download a QR code reader app that is made specifically for your phone or tablet brand.

Videos may also be accessed at https://resources.corwin.com/tenminuteprincipal

PREFACE

THE CHALLENGE AHEAD

Like many who enter the profession of education, I wanted to do my best. I was a happy and contented classroom teacher, and my students improved as readers and writers. When offered an administrative job, I thought I could manage the transition. Certainly, administration would be similar to leading a class of students. I was wrong. Quickly, old memories of my days in school returned.

On the night before I started high school, I lay wide-awake in my bed. Staring at the ceiling, I felt scared and excited, and I wondered whether I would find friends and do well in my classes. Now as I reflect on that night, specific details have faded away, but those anxious feelings remain.

The old fearful thoughts I felt the night before high school returned the evening prior to my first day of being a school principal. I felt a sense of wonder as I thought about leading a school. But the emotion that dominated and replayed in my mind was the same fear I experienced the night before I started high school. Was I ready for the journey I was about to take? I wasn't sure.

Finally, I was able to push negative thoughts from my mind and think about my success in graduate school and the mentors I had when I was assistant principal of a junior high school. Fears and worries battled with wonder and excitement because I realized that as the principal, others would look to me to make decisions and provide guidance, support, and leadership. The responsibility, the enormity of the task, overtook my thoughts. Just as I did before starting high school, the evening before my first day as principal, I stared at the ceiling in my room. Sleep wouldn't come. What truly worried me was that my fears seemed reasonable.

While I lay awake, one specific thought bombarded my mind, a thought that rings true to this day. For my school to develop a positive and collaborative culture, have a staff and students who look forward to coming every day, and have parent and community support, my leadership would be needed. Reasons for a lack of success would be my failures. I had big challenges to face and address, as well as a legit reason to feel nervous. Nevertheless, the first morning I walked into school as the principal, I walked in determined to build a successful learning community.

THE JOURNEY BEGINS

Being an effective administrator can be challenging. I quickly found myself reacting to situations instead of planning a successful path forward. At one time or another, like me, you might find yourself reacting to events instead of being proactive. It's important to keep this idea in your mind: Continually reacting to situations (instead of following your plan) is a roadblock to success.

During my first year as a principal and for many years after, I wished for a book to help me gain insights and offer ideas on how to do the following:

- Prioritize my time
- Build better relationships with staff and students
- Make teaching and learning a primary focus
- Collaboratively shape the culture in my school

My hope is *The Ten-Minute Principal* will help you avoid many of the errors I made. I don't have it all figured out and continue to learn every day. However, experiencing fifteen years on the job, reading professional materials, and having conversations with other administrators and teachers have all taught me a great deal. Note, too, that there are no magic fixes, and it isn't possible to be a successful principal in ten minutes. Ten-minute opportunities occur several times during the day. As you read on, you'll explore ways to refine your craft and become a reflective and intentional thinker and leader.

Ten minutes. Short intervals of time allow you to focus on the diverse needs that arise all day for students, staff, parents, and community. These ten-minute opportunities can occur during each day of the year. I will be sharing how ten minutes of focused time can improve your leadership, effectiveness, and, ultimately, your school.

FEATURES OF THE BOOK

Throughout the book you will find these recurring features:

- #10MinutePrincipal (key points to remember)
- 10-Minute Opportunities

- ■ 10-Minute Tips
- ■ 10-Minute Collaboration suggestions
- ■ Vignettes from education leaders offering reflections on how to improve leadership
- ■ End-of-chapter 10-Minute Reflections on Opportunities for Change
- ■ End-of-chapter podcasts that elaborate on the main points of the chapter

10-Minute Opportunities: Notice I use the word *opportunity.* As you explore ideas in this book, I encourage you to view challenges as opportunities. This is a subtle shift that can impact your outlook and set a good example for staff and students. Each chapter has several ten-minute opportunities for you to consider, as well as reflective questions and suggestions that can lead to positive changes.

10-Minute Tips: Every chapter will have several ten-minute tips. I include these to help you navigate a challenge with the understanding that your time is valuable.

10-Minute Collaboration suggestions: School leaders expect students and staff to collaborate. Each chapter will offer suggestions for collaborating with students, staff, or parents to address challenges that inevitably come your way. It's helpful to remember the old saying "It takes a team to find success; failure can be done alone."

A QUICK CHAPTER OVERVIEW

I have organized *The Ten-Minute Principal* so you can easily access information. You can read the book from cover to cover or go to specific sections in each chapter based on your needs or interests.

Chapter 1. The Six Pillars of School Leadership. I have pulled together six aspects of leadership that have been my guide and called them the six pillars of leadership: vision, relationships, trust, efficacy, a student-centered environment, and instructional knowledge. In Chapter 1, I discuss and connect each pillar to leadership, knowing that as you deal with daily challenges, they will support your interactions and collaboration with staff and students and enable you to build a positive and inclusive school culture.

Chapter 2. The Principal, Communication, and School Culture. Here, you will find ideas on communication and school culture. Schools that have positive, learning-focused cultures do not happen by accident—they are created. Communication is the key to establishing a positive culture. You'll explore how to create a culture that is positive and student focused.

Chapter 3. Relationship Building. Relationships are a foundation of effective classrooms and schools. You'll explore strategies to cultivate partnerships without compromising what you believe. I will guide you through detailed information on the importance of relationships and provide ten-minute strategies to help you cultivate and enhance relationships with students, staff, and parents.

Chapter 4. Purposeful Meetings. I used to dread meetings but not anymore. Meetings are opportunities to model behaviors, communicate expectations, problem solve, and work collaboratively with staff and students. The ten-minute strategies show you how to organize and lead meetings, as well as how to model classroom best practices through meetings.

Chapter 5. Fostering Creativity. Educators often hear, read, or discuss the importance of creativity and creative problem solving. In this chapter, you'll reflect on ideas and suggestions for enhancing or creating a school culture focused on creativity, innovation, and growth mindset.

Chapter 6. Choose Your Path. This chapter will ask you to reflect on where you have been, where you are, and where your future path might go. In addition, there will be suggestions on how to handle challenges that aren't working and ways to measure your success.

As you read and reflect on the six pillars of school leadership in Chapter 1, I'm hoping they will guide you and your staff as you collaborate to create a trusting and positive school culture. Moreover, the six pillars can support you as you work daily to make a difference in the lives of every student and member of your school's staff.

The following resources are available through the companion website (https://resources.corwin.com/ tenminuteprincipal).

 Video 2.1 Cougar News Clip
https://resources.corwin.com/tenminuteprincipal

 Podcast 2.1 Words and Actions
https://resources.corwin.com/tenminuteprincipal

 Podcast 3.1 Accentuate the Positive
https://resources.corwin.com/tenminuteprincipal

 Podcast 4.1 School Initiatives
https://resources.corwin.com/tenminuteprincipal

 Podcast 5.1 Mindset Matters
https://resources.corwin.com/tenminuteprincipal

 Podcast 6.1 Your Path
https://resources.corwin.com/tenminuteprincipal

ACKNOWLEDGMENTS

The poet John Donne wrote, "No man is an island." Although I wrote *The Ten-Minute Principal* myself, others were there to support my efforts. First, I must thank my wife, Cookie, who took over our shared household chores to provide me with more time to write. Most importantly, she encouraged me and had faith in my ability to write a book that would resonate with other leaders.

Many thanks to my mother, Laura Robb, who believed I had an important message to offer others.

To the staff and students of my school, who daily inspire me to be a better educator and do the best I can for kids, my sincere thanks!

Finally, I appreciate and thank the Corwin staff who offered helpful editorial guidance and suggestions that added clarity and depth to the book.

PUBLISHER'S ACKNOWLEDGMENTS

Corwin gratefully acknowledges the contributions of the following peer reviewers:

Lydia Adegbola
English Department Chairperson, High School
New Rochelle, NY

Rich Hall
Director of Elementary Education
Richmond, VA

Angela M. Mosley
Administrator
Henrico, VA

Tanna Nicely
Executive Principal, Elementary
Knoxville, TN

Debra Paradowski
Associate Principal, High School
Hartland, WI

Angela Thompson
Assistant Director of Professional Learning and Leadership
Richmond, VA

ABOUT THE AUTHOR

Evan Robb is the principal of Johnson-Williams Middle School in Berryville, Virginia. He has over twenty years of experience serving as a building-level principal, including opening a junior high school in Warren County, Virginia. Prior to being a school principal, he was an English teacher, department chair, and assistant principal. Early in his career, Evan received the Horace Mann Educator of the Year Award. In addition, the NCTE Commission on Reading selected him to serve on its board.

Evan leads sustainable change initiatives that transform school culture, increase achievement, and prepare students for their future. In addition to being a full-time principal, Evan speaks across the country on leadership, how to improve literacy in schools, the digital principal, social media, how to involve all staff in goal setting, how to organize effective work teams, and the impact of culture and positivity on work.

His first book, *The Principal's Leadership Sourcebook: Practices, Tools, and Strategies for Building a Thriving School Community*, was published by Scholastic in the fall of 2007. Explore The Robb Review Education Blog at www.therobbreviewblog.com for more of his thoughts on teaching, learning, and leadership. The Robb Review Education Blog focuses on looking ahead, not looking back. Evan also has a podcast, www.therobbreviewpodcast.podbean.com. He has been named one of the top twenty-five educational leaders to follow on Twitter (@ERobbPrincipal; Kemp, 2018).

1

THE SIX PILLARS OF SCHOOL LEADERSHIP

T he six pillars of leadership evolved over my twenty years serving as an assistant principal and principal. By working through staff, student, parent, and instructional challenges,

I developed the six pillars and always keep them in the forefront of my mind:

1. Vision
2. Relationships
3. Trust
4. Efficacy
5. A student-centered environment
6. Instructional knowledge

I believe the pillars work in concert to form a solid and lasting leadership foundation. They are guideposts for you, and as you build and reinforce each one, you also can develop them in all members of your school community. The pillars enable you to develop a positive school culture that values taking risks, encouraging kindness, raising questions, practicing collaboration, and using communication. The pillars also encourage school community members to view problems as challenges and support one another. They help us recognize that the students we serve deserve to learn in a student-focused environment that values and respects their needs but also works diligently to meet those needs.

My hope is that as you read about the six pillars of leadership they will resonate with you as much as they do with me. They have become my beacon and lead my thinking and reactions as I navigate daily challenges and celebrate the positives I notice. I'm hoping they will become your leadership compass.

The pillars form the foundation of leadership and developing a creative and innovative school culture. It's helpful to reflect on each pillar and how your school integrates the pillar into every aspect of school life. Frequent reflection on the pillars, the challenges you face, and initiatives you're juggling can help you become a proactive leader. Deep reflection brings understanding,

Figure 1.1   The Six Pillars

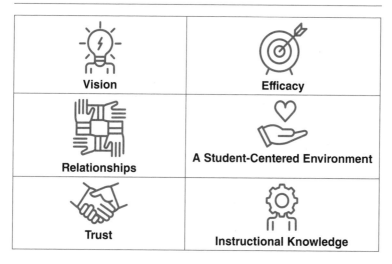

Vision	Efficacy
Relationships	A Student-Centered Environment
Trust	Instructional Knowledge

and it's possible to change or adjust what you understand. Be intentional with your time. Effective leaders intentionally carve out quiet moments to reflect in order to gain insight into myriad problems and challenges faced every day.

Be intentional with your time. #10MinutePrincipal

THE FIRST PILLAR: VISION

If you want to build a ship, then don't drum up men to gather wood, give orders, and divide the work. Rather, teach them to yearn for the far and endless sea.

—Antoine de Saint-Exupéry (*The Little Prince,* 1959)

When the principal uses imagination and creativity to develop with staff a clear and concise vision, it's possible to move beyond today's needs and imagine the "far and endless sea." A school's vision statement is best when it's concise, clear, and explains where the school is heading. Included in your vision statement should be its purpose and the commitments needed to take the journey. One characteristic of effective leadership is for you to collaborate with staff to develop a clear vision.

Starbucks has an excellent example of a vision statement: "Establish Starbucks as the premier purveyor of the finest coffee in the world while maintaining our uncompromising principles as we grow" (Starbucks, n.d.). Starbucks communicates a clear and action-focused vision statement; effective schools do the same. Moreover, vision statements work for the present, but also reach for the future.

My school's vision statement is an example of meeting present needs but working toward future needs, stating, "Each child is given the opportunity to succeed in a nurturing, positive, and flexible environment created by all staff." The statement focuses staff's energy on continuous instructional improvement to meet the ever-changing needs of students.

To collaboratively create a vision for your school, ask and reflect on these questions: *What does your school want to be? How will you get there? How can you inspire others to take this journey?* Your ultimate goal is to develop a collective vision by listening to the comments, questions, and stories of your staff.

Building a Collective Vision

To develop a collective vision among all or most staff, collaborate and create common goals linked to the vision, revisit and adjust goals often, and hold ongoing conversations to assess the staff's needs. Once you are aware of these needs, you can support staff through providing professional development, studying professional articles, and visiting other schools. A clear collective vision allows you to make decisions, organize shared initiatives, and hire staff aligned with your vision and the school's beliefs.

Your role is to keep the vision alive by communicating it, sharing stories about staff members who exemplify it, and integrating the vision into instructional conversations. Remember, it is always important for you to ask or personally consider whether your decisions, teachers' decisions, or groups' decisions connect to your school's vision. When actions repeatedly don't coordinate with your communicated vision, the vision's meaning wanes, and staff might stop using it as an instructional beacon.

THE SECOND PILLAR: RELATIONSHIPS

The most important single ingredient in the formula of success is knowing how to get along with people.

—Teddy Roosevelt

Education is about human interaction, communication, and connections. Think relationships, relationships, relationships! As Roosevelt points out, success depends on how people get along with each other. So the big question is *How do you foster positive relationships among staff?* One experience that enabled me to build better relationships among grade-level teams was to invite teachers to explore ways to find time during the day to work collaboratively on developing project-based learning experiences. You'll find that when you combine clear expectations and turn some leadership over to teachers, relationships build as well as commitment to the initiative. You can reflect on other ways to have teachers collaborate, such as working with the librarian on updating the collection or with a technology resource teacher to find effective ways for technology to enhance project-based learning. When positive, professional relationships coordinate with your school's vision, community develops and success follows. This happens when you share your leadership vision and turn part of the process over to staff.

Relationship Building

Savvy educators know that students don't learn from teachers who they perceive don't like them. The same is true for teachers who resist cooperating with you when they perceive you dislike them. Consider the suggestions in Figure 1.2 for relationship building among staff and students.

Avoid using your positional authority to compel students or staff to comply with a scheduling or instructional decision. Sometimes top-down decisions are tempting because they appear easy. But the fallout from such decisions can take months to repair. Instead, build relationships and trust to create a community committed to supporting your school's vision.

For example, if you want teachers to risk trying new instructional strategies such as inquiry and project-based learning, they need to feel comfortable taking risks. They need to believe that you support them and recognize that mistakes may be part of their best efforts. Your staff's risk taking is highly dependent on how they internalize your communications about risk taking and their observations of you taking risks. If your leadership builds trust and positive relationships, a result can be strong confidence among staff and a willingness to be innovative and creative (Kouzes & Posner, 2006).

Figure 1.2   Relationship Building With Staff and Students

Relationship Building: Staff	Relationship Building: Students
Be an active listener. Listen with the intent of understanding instead of just responding.	Invest time to get to know all students in the building: Be visible when classes change or in the lunchroom, always ready for quick exchange.
Communicate your expectations clearly.	Give specific praise to students when teachers point out their progress.
Be visible in the school and accessible in your office.	Offer specific praise when you observe good behavior.
Continue to get to know your staff as individuals.	Help students understand that they have hope for improving.
Demonstrate positivity in your words and actions.	Have diverse ways for students to connect to the school, such as extracurricular activities and leadership roles.
Strive to be honest and transparent.	Establish formal ways to hear students' opinions, such as a principal–students leadership team.
Attend school functions.	Encourage teachers to display students' work around the building.

 ## THE THIRD PILLAR: TRUST

When we tell people to do their jobs, we get workers. When we trust people to get the job done, we get leaders.

—Simon Sinek (2009)

Relationships are the foundation of trust. When you nurture positive relationships, trust develops. When you help staff and students feel safe at school, when you value their thinking and respect them as individuals, you create a trusting school culture. Simon Sinek (2009) implies that if you trust yourself to nurture positive relationships in your school, you demonstrate a leadership style that focuses on others and values collaboration, communication, and consensus building.

If you make top-down decisions, know that turmoil among staff may occur and trust can diminish. For example, project-based learning (PBL) is certainly a popular instructional method. The question for you to consider is *How can I bring PBL into my building in a manner that builds trust?*

A top-down administrator announces that all teachers will start a PBL project in October, and students will share with other classes at the end of November. Consider the negative impact on trust of top-down decision-making and whether it truly impacts instructional change (most likely, it doesn't). To accomplish this type of innovative practice, it would be better to explore how much your staff members know about PBL, to include staff in professional learning offered, and then give teachers the choice of starting and ending dates. Not only does this increase trust among staff, but it also showcases your inclusive leadership style and encourages taking risks.

The vision of preparing students for their future (not our past) cannot be met if staff are afraid to try new things. You can foster trusting relationships among and between staff and students by making collaborative decisions that can lead to teachers trying current research-based practices. If you want a new and different result in using technology to enhance students' learning, support your staff with training. But for staff to try new techniques requires risk, a change in their mindset, and modeling by you. When you encourage staff to take risks by making them feel supported and part of the decision-making process, they in turn feel safe to try new methods.

Let me give you an example. It's interesting that the chairman of JetBlue, in his book on leadership (Peterson & Kaplan, 2016), chose trust as a way to build bonds among workers and to improve corporate culture and customer service. The same is true of schools. A goal of JetBlue was to build high trust because it leads to altruistic decisions and success. For you to create a high-trust school, your decisions need to be in the best interest of students. In addition, your staff need to feel safe and understand they aren't working in a school with a "gotcha" environment. Important to remember: How you manage trust directly affects all members of your school community.

 ## THE FOURTH PILLAR: EFFICACY

They are able who think they are able.

—Virgil

Efficacy is the belief that you and I can make a difference in the lives of students we work with every day. Point out a school where all teachers have high efficacy, and I'll wager their staff and administration are working to meet all students' needs. As Virgil told us more than two thousand years ago, if you believe you can effect change, you will find ways to inspire others to join you.

There are two kinds of efficacy schools need: individual efficacy and collective efficacy. A combination of both can result in staff, administration, students, and parents developing and sustaining a mindset that focuses on making a difference in every aspect of school life. Fostering individual efficacy in your school community starts with you. By developing efficacy within yourself, by reading about and discussing efficacy at team, department, and full faculty meetings, and by integrating it into daily interactions with staff and students, you hold the key to changing and strengthening an individual's efficacy.

Individual Efficacy

When professionals believe it's possible to make a difference in how students learn, show their school spirit, and display their citizenship, they seek new ways to enhance their skills and improve their job performance. Such educators see them-selves as learners who want to develop as professionals and explore new ways of teaching and interacting with students, colleagues, parents, and administrators. They understand and accept that all students don't learn new skills at the same time or pace. Equally important, they adjust curriculum to students' needs and provide support. Staff and administrators with these characteristics almost always have a strong sense of efficacy.

Administrators who have strong efficacy can affect the efficacy of the entire school community—teachers, staff, students, parents, and other administrators. Teachers with strong efficacy can develop efficacy among their students. Faith in the capacity of students and the belief in themselves to make a difference will always be common traits of great teachers. In addition, great teachers work diligently to improve their practice by reading professional materials, observing other teachers, and discussing ideas with like-minded colleagues.

However, an even greater impact is the efficacy of an entire staff—when all and not just a few dedicate themselves to students' success and believe they can make a difference for each student in their school.

Collective Efficacy

This moves from the individual to all staff in a school or, even better, in a school division. When all staff believe they can impact learning and help students find success, then every student can improve. John Hattie has conducted a meta-analysis of what factors most influence student achievement. With an effect size of 1.57, collective total efficacy is ranked as the *number-one* factor influencing student achievement (Hattie, 2016). Just as with school culture, collective efficacy does not happen by accident. For collective efficacy to take hold in a school, it must be led by the principal. Research has clearly proven that students learn and achieve better in schools that have staff with high collective efficacy.

Every student who attends school in America or any other country deserves a teacher and a school that believes in his or her capacity to learn and grow. Let me bring this back to you: It is impossible to find a school with high collective efficacy led by a principal who does not believe and, most importantly, communicate the same.

THE FIFTH PILLAR: A STUDENT-CENTERED ENVIRONMENT

There is an emphasis on doing things right rather than on doing the right things.

—Thomas Sergiovanni (1992)

Put students at the center of your thinking when developing a student-centered environment. Equally important is for you to find opportunities to include students in some decisions. For example, when planning a school spirit week, if you and teachers decide what will happen, most likely students won't buy into the plan. However, you can use students' suggestions gathered from a student leadership group, review their ideas, develop and conduct a survey among students, and then use the top results for your spirit week.

I have known teachers who believed they were doing things right, but their notion of right wasn't always best for students. I recall a science teacher who planned his lessons, tests, assignments, and homework for the entire school year—definitely not student-centered. He stressed out when we missed school for a snow day because it messed up the sequence of his lessons. This is an extreme example, but I share it with you to point out that rigidity has little place in education. Rigid educators are not student-centered. Student-centered teachers certainly plan in advance, but they know plans are not written in stone. What they do know is that plans change based on the formative data gathered from students each day. All day long, you'll be making decisions that affect the environment and culture of your school. Be thoughtful and take time.

When you approach decision-making, you need to ask yourself these questions: *Are my decisions good for students? Am I helping teachers understand the WHY behind my decisions?* In

Figure 1.3   Strategies for Developing a Student-Centered Environment

Principal's Student Leadership Opportunities	Teachers' Student-Centered Instructional Practices
Create an appointed student leadership council.	Differentiate instruction with an emphasis on choice.
Have an elected student government.	Use learning style inventories.
Train a student news team.	Use flexible seating negotiated between the teacher and students.
Create student mentoring opportunities.	Negotiate deadlines.
Develop peer mediation programs.	Retake and redo opportunities.
Promote community service opportunities.	Evaluate grading based on mastery.
Organize a National Honor Society program.	Do self-evaluation and peer editing.
Create a student ambassador program to assist with after-school functions.	Include genius hour opportunities.
Provide opportunities for students to work on the school's yearbook and literary magazine.	Offer project-based learning.

a student-centered environment, you make decisions that are in the best interests of students. Here's a classic example that occurs during testing time. Do you design the schedule for students' success? Or do you design a schedule that appeases faculty by keeping planning periods intact? A student-centered school adopts Sergiovanni's (1992) position, and you and teachers collaborate to make decisions that are best for students. In Figure 1.3, you will find some student leadership options and instructional practices you can consider when working with staff to develop a student-centered environment. However, if your staff need to transition from teacher-centered to student-centered, you will need to provide ongoing professional learning for this change to occur.

By now, I'm sure you see similarities when comparing a classroom to a school. A rigid classroom and a flexible learner-focused classroom both impact learning, as well as the school's environment and culture. In general, compliance, strict rules, rigid grading systems, and limited instructional methods define rigid school structures. In contrast, student-centered schools embrace collaborative ways of learning, are inclusive, creative, innovative, and emphasize the importance of instructional knowledge.

THE SIXTH PILLAR: INSTRUCTIONAL KNOWLEDGE

The mind is not a vessel to be filled, but a fire to be ignited.

—Plutarch

Instructional knowledge includes strategies teachers can use to engage and motivate students in their learning. There's a wide range of instructional strategies that work across the curriculum, such as inquiry learning, discussion groups, book clubs, integrating technology to enhance learning, and offering choice in reading, projects, and writing topics. These are but a few, and it's your responsibility to ensure that teachers have a range and depth of knowledge of instructional strategies so they can integrate them into lessons. If not, instruction will mirror their personal experiences.

I was a great history student—at least, this is what I thought of myself every Friday when I was in high school. The year was 1983. Each week was the same in my class: notes on Monday and Tuesday with accompanying lectures; Wednesday was worksheet day; and Thursday we played games to prepare us for the Friday multiple-choice test. Some students did well, and some did not. But each week ended with a test, and the following Monday we moved forward.

Thirty-five years later was my first year as principal of my current school. There I was, in a history classroom, doing an observation of a revered veteran staff member. Notes, lectures, and (as I learned during our post-observation meeting) tests every Friday—no different from what I'd experienced more than thirty-five years before. All school leaders need to understand that our students deserve better.

If your goal is to light the fire of learning among students in your school, you need to embrace ongoing learning for yourself and your staff. The principal as instructional leader and a staff of followers can never be as strong as a school where the principal encourages instructional leadership among all staff. Carrying the weight of being the only instructional leader or the "expert" on instructional knowledge is too large a burden, and it does not empower others to grow. Seek out ways to share leadership by growing capacity in others. Moreover, by committing to the growth of your staff, you empower them to have a positive impact on students.

According to Michael Fullan (2010), "Successful principals develop others in a way that is integrated into the work of the school" (p. 14). You hold the power to create a culture in which you are the leader among leaders or among followers and resisters. As an instructional leader, your primary goal is to develop the instructional capacity of every teacher through conversations, observations, professional learning, and staff sharing what works for them. It's the principal's job to have pedagogical knowledge but also to inspire staff to become ongoing learners. The question to reflect on is *How does the principal accomplish this?* My suggestion is to continually assess your school's performance, look at data indicators, and have conversations with staff to determine instructional needs. To reach this goal each school year, I suggest you develop with staff a coordinated professional development plan that addresses the needs of your building. This has to occur annually since needs will change.

As your school's instructional leader, it's key to always address and improve the state of the six pillars. If the six pillars are strong and you inspire staff to improve and refine their craft, then they will most likely accept the additional effort required to improve instruction. Here are a few suggestions for targeted professional development based on the needs of your building. The suggestions that follow can enable you to achieve the goals you and your staff have agreed upon, which can be addressed during scheduled faculty meetings, professional development days, and team and department meetings:

- Engage a professional consultant over a period of time to provide support in your building to your staff. Doing this means everyone receives training.
- Form expert groups among your staff so people can learn from each other.

- Organize books and/or professional article studies with discussion, reflection, and application opportunities.
- Encourage and model how professional learning networks through social media can enhance professional learning.

The principal and administrative team should attend all building-level professional learning and send the message that improvement, learning, and change are for all school staff. In addition, it's crucial for the principal and other administrators to have a deep understanding of instructional changes so they can purchase materials and know what to look for when visiting classrooms.

At the end of the day, you want to develop teachers who bring something unique to your school. You might think like this: If you have a dinner party and each person is asked to bring something, some will bring a great homemade dish, others will purchase a side of coleslaw, and a few won't bring anything.

CLOSING THOUGHTS

You want people on your team who bring something special to your table, your school. And those who bring little? You will need to think hard on this because what others see you as tolerant of gives them permission to do the same. When you work with staff to integrate the six pillars into every aspect of school life, you create a positive, consensus-building school culture.

The six pillars are the foundation for *The Ten-Minute Principal* and our journey together.

10-MINUTE REFLECTIONS ON OPPORTUNITIES FOR CHANGE

- How does your leadership style include some or all of the six pillars?
- Can you pinpoint an area that you can work on with staff (such as being more inclusive, improving communication)? What might be your first steps?
- Are you and staff thinking with a student-first mindset? Are there changes that can occur through conversations and planning together?

Note: The 6 Pillars icons in this chapter are from iStock.com/fleaz.

2

THE PRINCIPAL, COMMUNICATION, AND SCHOOL CULTURE

Effective schools have a positive school culture and established communication norms to keep students, staff, and parents informed. A school's culture is the sum of the values, beliefs, traditions, and actions of all staff. If a building is student focused, this speaks to school culture. If a school values traditional, teacher-centered methods of instruction, this, too, speaks to its culture. If the principal is inclusive, the school will likely develop a consensus-building culture. Of course, if the principal is autocratic, the school will likely have a culture of anxiety and compliance.

Considering school culture reminded me of a recent conversation with my mother, Laura Robb, who speaks and consults on reading and writing across the country. On my way home from work, we discussed two workshops she had completed for different schools. One school was unwelcoming; it lacked vitality and the staff was apathetic. The other school she described as "awesome." She could sense the positive feelings. She felt welcome. Staff were upbeat and excited to be at school. Students seemed happy, and teachers posted their work around the school. You can probably guess the next question I asked my mother: Was the principal present at both of her workshops? I felt confident I knew what the answer would be, and I was correct. In the school where teachers weren't invested in the workshop, the principal was nowhere to be seen. However, in the school with upbeat teachers who wanted to learn, the principal actively participated with teachers for the entire half-day workshop.

> **Leadership by example can have a positive impact if what is being modeled is beneficial for students and staff. #10MinutePrincipal**

So what does this mean for you? And what does it mean for a school's culture and communication? It means a lot. You are the communicator and flag bearer of your school's culture. To achieve this alignment, staff should observe consistency between your words and actions.

The school level is one example. The same is true for a classroom in any school in America. Show me a class that is dynamic and student-centered with engaged and motivated students, and that class will be led by a teacher who fosters and models those same characteristics. Leadership by example can have a positive impact if what is being modeled is beneficial for students and staff. As you continue to read, you will explore how communication creates a culture of excellence within a school or in a classroom.

E-MAIL: I NEED SOME STRATEGIES

I have come a long way with my use of e-mail as a communication tool. Today, it is hard for me to recall how I managed work early in my career when e-mail was new in schools. Managing e-mail and learning how to communicate effectively through it is important for you and your staff.

A primary goal of this book is transparency, allowing you to understand my beliefs and why they have changed. In addition to sharing positive experiences, I will also recount some events that didn't work well. What follows is one such example.

My first administrative job was in 1997, and I was an assistant principal. E-mail was new to my school. Using e-mail didn't interest me. My fixed mindset supported an avoidance of using e-mail for the first seven months of my job. Here is the odd part of this situation. Seven months into the job the superintendent asked to meet with me. When I walked into the office the next day, the superintendent leaned forward at his desk and said words I recall today: "Evan, you are so focused on doing a good job you don't have time to use e-mail. I admire it and want you to apply for a principal's position with us today." Well, I was dumbfounded but quickly agreed that I was too focused on my work to refine e-mail skills. I applied for the job, and two weeks later became a junior high school principal. Oddly enough, the conversation was the key motivator for me to start using technology at work, of course, including e-mail. Today, it is tough to imagine communication without e-mail. However, there can be challenges.

Expectations are important for teachers to communicate to students, and they are important for you to communicate to your school community. Less-than-clear expectations cause confusion. As you jot down notes, each of the questions should have an answer. Equally important, staff should know what your answers are because you have modeled them.

Consider (in Figure 2.1) an example from my school's faculty handbook for consistent e-mail signatures:

Figure 2.1   Example of a Consistent E-Mail Signature

Mr. Evan A. Robb, MBA
Principal, Johnson-Williams Middle School
200 Swan Avenue
Berryville, VA 22611
540–955–6160
jwms.clarke.k12.va.us
Follow me on Twitter, Facebook, and Instagram.

"Encourage Inspire Empower"

A school's professional image is important for the school and its staff. When corresponding with e-mail, the professional image improves when staff uses a consistent format for signing. Notice how I use the signature to promote our social media, logo, and our division's mission.

Expectations are important for teachers. Less-than-clear expectations cause confusion. #10MinutePrincipal

 ## 10-MINUTE OPPORTUNITY

Take ten minutes to reflect on questions leading to a deeper understanding of how you use e-mail and model its use to staff.

- Have you communicated a standard for response time? If you have, do you model to staff and parents the standard you have set?
- Have you discussed with staff when e-mail should be used instead of picking up the phone to have a conversation?
- Does your school have additional standards in place, such as adding your professional picture to e-mail, applying a standard e-mail signature, always adding a subject, and never using all capitals when responding?
- Who should staff reach out to if they are not sure how to respond to an e-mail?

10-MINUTE TIP

Are teachers in your school using e-mail to update parents about learning and events such as plays and projects? Weekly teacher updates are a great communication tool as long as everyone commits to doing it. If one or several staff send weekly e-mails to parents and others don't, parents receiving no communication can rightfully raise concerns. To get all teachers on board, collaborate to establish expectations and set up support systems, such as pairing team members strong in a particular skill with those who may not be as strong. If your building has a technology resource teacher, this person can also assist. Teachers are at diverse levels with instructional and technological skills. It's important to help each teacher feel valued and recognize that help is always available. For example, my school agreed that all teachers would have their own Google site. I worked with my technology resource teacher to establish Level 1 and Level 2 criteria. Level 1 is a basic site, and Level 2 a more advanced site. Together, we worked with staff to develop a timeline for each level. In concert with these expectations, we worked with staff to discover their support needs.

Here's my tip: When you initiate new ways to communicate, make sure staff agree to consistency. If not, parents will look to you for answers and action. Coordinated and planned staff initiatives are always good practice. Now, what I am about to say is true time and again, and it will be restated in this book: _Staff and parents will judge you by what you are willing to tolerate._ If you tolerate sporadic communication or inconsistent use of communication, consider what this tells others about you as a leader and professional.

Staff and parents will judge you by what you are willing to tolerate. #10MinutePrincipal

 ## 10-MINUTE COLLABORATION

Create collaborative opportunities to communicate in new ways to parents: Try video for your weekly updates! I recall the Friday folders my own children brought home from elementary school at the end of each week—large folders with samples of academic work as well as school informa- tion. In my house, no one looked at the Friday folder until Sunday night!

Over time, I have seen many iterations of weekly com- munications: teacher weekly e-mails, team e-mails, and newsletters. In general, most were OK, but far from great. My challenge to you is seek out some adventurous staff members and together create and pilot new ways to inform families. Take the leap and try video for you and teachers to update families. Informing families about school life through videos provides a great example for others and will likely spawn more interest! A bi-monthly message from the prin- cipal's desk is a great starting place for you. This allows you to model the idea and at the same time better inform

(Continued)

(Continued)

parents. Videos created by phone or using a free Google extension called Screencastify are excellent tools. Consider making under-three-minute videos to e-mail to families, allowing you and other staff to connect in a new way! Finally, I recommend you make a commitment to captioning videos so hearing impaired parents can enjoy them, too.

E-mail and small videos improve communication and define to families the value you and staff place on communication. I have often posted a short video on social media (Facebook or Twitter) addressing families in preparation for the new school year. I hope you too will be inspired to explore ways to increase communication and build your school's brand.

BUILD YOUR SCHOOL'S BRAND

How do you build the brand of your school? How does branding connect to culture and communication? This may be an odd question. Most of us associate the word *brand* with something we like—a restaurant or a coffee shop. Right now, ask yourself, *Is there a restaurant in your area people always go to eat? Why?* Sometimes it can be the food, but other times, it is harder to define. Businesses use the word *buzz* to describe what draws people to them. The same feeling can be associated with your school. Consider some ways to create positive buzz and build your brand by cultivating school spirit among students, staff, families, and the greater community.

Branding or marketing schools to your community should be part of every school's action plan. Each school has unique stories to tell about staff, students, academics, sports, fine arts, technology programs, annual learning initiatives, special events, and so on. When schools reach out to parents and the community to tell their stories, they brand their schools by celebrating all that's inspiring and excellent. Schools committed to branding efforts build parent and community confidence and pride. Moreover, well-branded schools provide additional benefits to an area, possibly drawing in people desiring to purchase a house and/or run a business near the school.

To avoid making branding overly complex, I suggest starting with this goal: View branding as aligning what you want people to think about your school (and division) with what people actually think. This involves choosing the stories to tell that move a school closer to congruency. If a disconnect exists between reality and people's perceptions, view this as an opportunity to take action and improve.

I recall the day I met with my superintendent to let him know I wanted to make a concerted effort to build our school's brand. I shared my ideas of logo promotion, use of social media, and video to better communicate our message and inform families of special events. Though the superintendent was somewhat cautious about my ideas, he was supportive, so I moved forward. First, I organized a team that included the librarian, a teacher connected to social media, and myself. Together, we decided on a multipronged strategy. We recommended logo promotion through signage, on clothing, and a coordinated use of social media (Twitter, Instagram, and Facebook). In addition, we'd use video to record school events for families and introduce a twice-a-month news show run by a student news team who collaborated with me.

These strategies had an immediate impact on our communications and started to redefine the culture of our school. Building your school's brand can have the same impact if you make it a priority. Remember, you'll get results where you put your effort. It is often the main reason initiatives succeed or fail.

A few years ago my school had a challenge getting students to dress for P.E. Through student conversations, we pinpointed the problem: Students disliked how our logo looked on a gym uniform. Working with P.E. staff, we organized a redesign-the-logo contest, and students selected a new logo for gym uniforms. Quickly, the dressing-for-gym problem vanished.

Your website, letterhead, clothing, and wall murals are just a few of the many ways to promote the brand of your school. Whether you keep or change your school's logo, set aside time and create a plan to review how your school currently promotes its logo and if the school could improve logo promotion. Your school logo can and should make a strong connection to students, staff, parents, and community members because this builds school spirit, which impacts school culture.

 10-MINUTE OPPORTUNITY

Is it time to redesign your school's logo? How are you promoting your school's logo? Logos need to appeal to students, especially if you want to use the school's logo on clothing. The first question to consider is this: *Does your school need to refresh its logo?* If so, consider promoting a school logo redesign contest.

To get this rolling, set up a ten-minute meeting with your art teacher or graphic design teacher to create guidelines for submissions and then develop a timeline, including when to announce the contest. After submissions are in, form a review panel of staff, students, and several parents to choose the winning design. Once the group selects a design, work with your team to promote the logo.

10-MINUTE TIP

Take ten minutes and review *some* of my social media expectations. Ask yourself, *Can these work in my school?* Promoting your school requires revisiting and reevaluating social media standards. This is a new and important responsibility of school leadership in the digital age.

Remember, everything you send out through social media should communicate the values of your school and division. Posts and images on social media should convey excitement, energy, and enthusiasm about your school, staff, students, and division. As staff interest grows, encourage them to promote social media through their professional accounts by using hashtags, retweets, and likes. Spread the message of all the exciting activities and events in your school!

Login Access

Limit who has login access to any social media account. Two or three staff who have access to a school Twitter or Instagram account is my recommendation. If one is absent, another can still send out information.

Give only one responsibility to the same person. Consider dividing up who manages each account.

Posting Frequency

Here are my recommendations for how frequently to post information to build your school's brand:

- At least three tweets each day
- At least one Facebook post per day
- At least one Instagram image per day
- At least one video per month

Start with two initiatives; I suggest Twitter and Instagram. Have a plan for when you'll add Facebook and video. Without a plan, this might not happen.

Important Tip! Establish an understanding of exactly what you promote and communicate on social media—control your message. If you only promote athletics, what will this tell others about what you value?

- Balance promotions among all activities—academic, athletic, fine arts, extracurricular clubs, and so on.
- Make sure you promote all aspects of your school.
- Communicate support and pride for other schools within your school district.

Communicating your school brand is part of the job of being a school leader. If you are not sure of the first step, look in the mirror and start with yourself. Yes! *You* should model everything you see as valuable, and social media can be a valuable communication tool for your school.

 10-MINUTE COLLABORATION

Develop and start a ten-minute video news program for students and parents!

A school news show might be the perfect next level for you, and ten minutes is the optimal length of such a video.

Several years ago, I invited students to apply for our school's news team. Students wrote a letter explaining why they wanted to be part of our school news show, and they each submitted a short video to highlight their budding newscasting skills. *Cougar* (our school mascot) *News* began and still continues as a wonderful work-in-progress with an ever-evolving format (see Figure 2.2). There is no perfect format for what makes a great school news show. In general, I suggest highlights of goings-on at school, interviews with teachers, and upcoming events as good starting points. In my school's newest version, we have two co-anchors, a technology reporter, and a sportscaster. My best advice is don't be rigid, have fun, and allow your students to be the dominant part of the news show. Let others shine!

(Continued)

(Continued)

Figure 2.2   Our School News Team

Source: Johnson-Williams Middle School (2018).
Our school news team! We do have fun, and this is our attempt to look like real news reporters.

Eric Sheninger, in his book *BrandEd* (2017), reminds us that if we don't tell our story, someone else will. Consider how you can use social media and video to better promote all the excellent things happening in your building. My technology resource teacher and I developed some suggestions for telling your school story.

SOCIAL MEDIA TIPS

Twitter Tips

- Push information out using your school's Twitter account. Keep in mind, every tweet in your feed (not just those you post) represents your school.

- Limit who has access; the school principal should be the main person running Twitter.
- Do not follow many people. Follow a Twitter account only after first tracking the tweets and posts on that account for a stretch of time.
- Retweet information other schools in your division share.
- Mention other schools from your division in your tweets. This can be done when you post or if you retweet information about another school or division.
- Mention your superintendent if he or she is on Twitter to further promote and communicate exciting goings-on in your school. By tagging someone's Twitter handle in your tweet, you ensure that it goes out to all of that person's followers as well as your own followers.

Facebook Tips

- Share images and video of all the exciting learning happening in your school on your school's Facebook page.
- Designate a staff member to populate content.
- Choose a staff member who monitors Facebook daily. In my school, the librarian runs and monitors our Facebook page.
- Include images and videos with accompanying text whenever possible.
- Keep parents and your community engaged by adding at least two posts per day.
- Moderate comments made by others. This means having to make the call to delete comments if they are inappropriate.

Instagram Tips

- Use hashtags and create your own hashtags to label images and drive viewers to your post.
- Post motivational images and captions on Instagram. You can also post pictures of events and learning activities from your school.

Video Tips

It takes some practice to create a good video product. As with Twitter, Instagram, and Facebook, it is important to set a standard of frequency and to stick to the plan. Don't set a schedule you cannot maintain. For a school news show, I suggest once or twice per month. This will give you time to meet and collaborate with your news team on topics each will speak to on the show.

- Wear clothing that makes you feel good about yourself.
- Watch your body language—everyone else will.
- Smile with your eyes.
- Use your hands to magnify your message.
- Use your natural voice.
- Pacing matters.

Take ten minutes to integrate at least one new strategy to enhance your public relations and build your school brand. Social media and video are powerful ways to tell your story. Never underestimate the power of your stories when building your school's brand. But also reserve time to consider the impression your front office staff make on visitors and your school community. For an example of how we do this at my school, watch Video 2.1, showcasing our student anchors on *Cougar News.*

Video 2.1 Cougar News Clip

 https://resources.corwin.com/tenminute principal

CUSTOMER SERVICE AND BUILDING A SCHOOL'S BRAND

Your front office staff offer the first impression of you and your school. I have known schools where front office staff are rude, demeaning, and at times yell at students while visitors wait to check in—not acceptable on any level. On the other hand, I have worked in and visited schools where the front office set an upbeat tone by connecting positively with students, staff, and families. Think about your school. How does your front office staff communicate and interact with teachers, students, parents, and visitors? Remember, the positive or negative impressions that office staff project directly reflect on your leadership.

Is your school brand committed to quality customer service or tolerant of less-than-stellar service? Both describe your school brand. #10MinutePrincipal

10-MINUTE OPPORTUNITY

Take ten minutes to reflect and take notes on my five indicators of good service:

1. Do students, staff, and parents feel welcome when entering the front office of your school?
2. Consider the visual impression the front office makes. Is it neat or messy?
3. Is your office staff friendly, patient, professional, and interested?
4. Do you have an office standard for answering the phone, taking messages, or placing a person on hold?
5. Is appropriate professional dress observable by you and others?

Your answers to these five questions can affirm quality service to school stakeholders or point out a need for change. Often when I discuss front office customer service with administrators, I am met with statements such as, "I don't have time in my day to handle this." My suggestion is to find time. I recall when I asked my wife for the telephone number of a school in our community, her response was, "You mean the school with that really rude secretary?" I am sure that principal did not have "time" to make some changes. Not taking time resulted in my wife's negative response. Remember, initiatives and practices in a school are a reflection of you, and they are part of defining the culture of your school. When you think of it that way, front office service cannot be overlooked.

10-MINUTE TIP

The ten-minute tip offers an easy way to start a conversation on service. To get going, call a morning office meeting, pose a question, and then take action.

Question: What are three to five customer service skills you think you collectively do well? I would like you all to reflect a few minutes first and then discuss and jot them down on paper. Next, list areas for office improvement.

Action: Set a date. You'll need three to four days to prepare for a ten-minute meeting to review the front office team's perception of their strengths and areas for improvement. Challenge office staff to improve by inviting them to set short- and long-term goals. Make clear that you will provide timely and specific feedback when you observe positive change.

10-MINUTE COLLABORATION

Good customer service results from frequent conversations if a high standard is to be maintained. I am sure you have been to a nice restaurant or hotel and experienced quality customer service. The quality you experience in these establishments does not happen by accident. The ten-minute collaboration offers ideas for your front office and your teaching staff to improve customer service.

Front Office

Does your division have a school with a highly professional front office? Send a member of your administrative team to that school. Have them observe, ask questions, and take notes about the school's front office protocols and service. Have your team member share with you and your front office team the new ideas to consider in a ten-minute debrief. After some reflection, invite your front office team to suggest ways they can use this idea to improve. This debrief will bring new ideas for your team to consider, allowing you to give feedback as they work to improve! Action should be taken shortly after debriefing and reflection. If not, sometimes people listen but do not make any changes.

Teaching Staff

Has your teaching staff established a time standard for returning a phone call or e-mail? Take ten minutes as part of a regularly scheduled meeting to ask staff if they have an agreed-upon standard for phone and e-mail response. Whenever I bring this up to staff, I get a scattered response; you may experience the same. Set a timeline for staff to discuss and agree on a standard. In my school, staff have agreed to a maximum of twenty-four hours to answer e-mails and same-day response for phone messages. Agreed-upon standards add to the professionalism of your team and in turn reflect positively on all members of your school community.

Action should be taken shortly after debriefing and reflection. If not, sometimes people listen but do not make any changes. #10MinutePrincipal

WHAT IS THE PRINCIPAL'S ROLE
IN BUILDING STRONG SCHOOL CULTURE?

Principal Dennis J. Schug Jr.
Hampton Bays Middle School
Hampton Bays, NY

I feel like I never know what's happening in there.
When I ask my kid how school was today, the response is always "Fine."
When I follow up with "Well, what did you do at school today?"
The answer I get is "Nothing."

These were the all-too-familiar words of parents of my students, and they represented my reality as a new principal in a new middle school. On the bright side, I was surrounded by hope, promise, and potential on the horizon—the best was yet to come. I was privileged to serve 650 amazing adolescents. And I was faced with the challenge to bridge gaps that existed in communication and in perceptions, based upon the communication divide between the typically complex phase called adolescence and caring parents wanting to learn what's going on in their ten-to-fourteen-year-olds' minds and hearts. And on the surface, this had quickly become my job as principal.

As the leader of the school, I had work to do—and our school culture depended on it. My goal was to foster a school of "We." Only together would we successfully shift perceptions from seeming like a school that doesn't

(Continued)

(Continued)

communicate openly to one in which we share a healthy school–home partnership.

I began by asking questions, with hopes that this would lead to a school culture we could all be proud of.

1. *How do we foster clear two-way communication in a way that can be easily accessed?*
2. *Where are our opportunities to collaborate and to both model and invite collaboration?*
3. *How can we sustain an open invitation to be an active member of our community of learners?*
4. *Where do opportunities exist to cultivate leadership among students, teachers, families, and community?*
5. *How can we model the value of relationships to promote constructive dialogue, coordinated efforts, and open and honest flow of ideas focused purely on students' academic achievement while being developmentally responsive?*

Working closely and intentionally with parents, teachers, and trusted mentors, I concluded that a healthy culture would best be achieved through multiple means. We hosted individual and small-group meetings at and away from school and at various times of the day. We outwardly promoted the various ways parents could reach us, and we were deliberate in learning how parents preferred to receive and share communication. Through daily social media posts, weekly e-mail blasts, and monthly in-person meetings, we shared, showcased, and celebrated our students' successes in everyday learning. I prioritized being both visible and present, in and out of classrooms and school events. The ultimate goal was to get back to basics, sitting face to face, side by side, working together, child by child. Being reliable, dependable, and even, to some degree, predictable is where, we discovered, trust is born.

Nearly a decade later, this has become a school community value. While we can never underestimate the role of trust in building a healthy school–home connection, it is the principal's job to meet people where they are to ensure that a two-way school–home relationship remains a priority.

PROFESSIONALISM: MODELING EXPECTATIONS, CULTURE, AND COMMUNICATION

Joe, an English teacher in my school, came by my office after school to complain. Joe just experienced a bad parent meeting, and he was upset. I asked Joe, "What happened?" Joe felt the parent was disrespectful and criticized him for being negative. We had a productive conversation about setting the stage for a meeting by sharing a mix of positives along with areas of student improvement and how parents can help. To this day, I can recall, at that very moment, my internal debate: *Should I tell him about his shirt or let it go?* I explained my thoughts this way: "Joe, I have shared some good strategies with you, and I know you want to be treated like a professional, but the shirt you have on says SPAM in big letters."

First impressions always count. Joe wanted to be treated like a professional, but he did not look like one. Moreover, he didn't plan the meeting so there would be positives about the student to offset the negatives. I've reflected on that meeting many times over the years. I had not communicated to Joe proper dress standards and how to organize a difficult meeting with parents. This encounter showed how much administrators set a school's tone. Joe's negative meeting was in part my fault. Remember, your expectations define a culture of a school as well as a classroom.

Excellent teachers know the value of negotiating and communicating positive expectations to students. Expectations become powerful in a classroom when they are part of class routines. Routines let students experience expectations negotiated with their teacher, and these form the foundation for classroom success.

Do you model and communicate expectations to students, staff, and parents? You represent your school. Your words, actions, and congruence between the two set the tone. Expectations and what you believe and do go hand in hand. Here are a few examples of expectations to communicate, promote, and champion:

- Believe in the capability of all students.
- Be a positive person.
- Embrace a growth mindset.
- Encourage creativity.
- Make student-centered decisions.
- Value and model being a learner.

- Give permission for purposeful risk taking.
- Support professional development, allowing technology to transform learning.
- Foster intentional, purposeful, and reflective teaching.
- Redefine the role of teacher, classroom space, and students.

The gain that occurs when you communicate your expectations and beliefs is that others learn what you are about and the level of professionalism you expect. Frequently, reread the expectations and ask yourself, *Could I better communicate my expectations and help staff to better understand my standards?* You can improve professionalism and positively impact your school's culture and communication by exploring the ten-minute opportunity that follows.

When people know what you stand for, they will be drawn to you or make a personal choice to go in a different direction. #10MinutePrincipal

 10-MINUTE OPPORTUNITY

If you feel some of your professional expectations need to change, remember it took time for those to develop. Change will not occur overnight. Change can take time and is always a process. What follows are the four questions I value and invite you to consider. Take ten minutes to reflect and jot notes on these.

- Could staff tell you the four or five expectations you value?

(Continued)

(Continued)

- Is there congruence between your expectations and actions?
- Do teachers communicate the school's expectations to students?
- What are concrete ways to foster professionalism among staff?

These are tough questions. Your answers can show you where to start. As you move from plans to taking action, you'll need to be sure others are receiving and understanding your message. Explore suggestions in the tips that follow.

 ## 10-MINUTE TIP

This ten-minute tip presents three ways you can better communicate you message. Try one and if that works, do another.

Faculty Meetings. Take ten minutes during each faculty meeting to review expectations and values. Invite staff to share an expectation they're implementing. For example, an expectation I communicate to staff is using technology to transform learning. Last year several teachers flipped their classroom for several units during the year. Flipping involved creating videos and/or screencasts of lessons that students could view at home. During a faculty meeting, invite staff who are effectively incorporating technology to share specific examples.

Video Message to Staff. Use a Chrome extension called Screencastify to make a video from your desk and e-mail it to staff. Video can be a good way to communicate expectations you and the school have been working on and also to add in several specific highlights. I have found this to be a convenient method to spread my message in between meetings. When using video to communicate to staff, always be positive and upbeat. No one appreciates a scolding on video. The video you send to staff should take no longer than three minutes. Even if you need a redo, this will take you no more than ten minutes.

Lead by Walking Around. Walking all parts of your school is a common method to gauge the pulse of an organization. You need to be seen, and visibility is another opportunity to talk with staff about expectations and values of the school. Personally, I prefer staff to be inundated with my message instead of never hearing it. When walking around your school, take time to give staff and students specific praise. Instead of saying, "Good use of technology in your class today," you might say, "As you know, transformative tech is a focus for our school. Your lesson was engaging and used technology in a way I have not seen before. Well done and keep it up!"

10-MINUTE COLLABORATION

Collaborate with staff and review expectations in your faculty handbook. If some statements require revision, ask for a small group to volunteer, rewrite, and bring

(Continued)

(Continued)

the revisions back to the staff for approval. Invite staff to review expectations in the faculty handbook annually (in addition to tweaking statements in the handbook)—you might want to add or delete one or two. Discuss and plan new expectations and values for the next school year. There are certainly times when you need to set the tone. There are also times when you and staff collaborate to create expectations and school values. And all the time, you grow your team and gain more traction. Engagement increases when plans are collaborative. Collaborations can be a ten-minute brainstorm during a meeting or part of informal communications with staff.

10-MINUTE REFLECTIONS
ON OPPORTUNITIES FOR CHANGE

- As you reflect on your school, what expectations are you modeling? How can you more effectively communicate your expectations and beliefs?
- Social media is a great way to tell your school's story. Are you using social media? What is your next level and timeline?
- Think about the word *professionalism*. Every school has some staff who have exemplary professional behavior and some staff who do not. How are you going to support those staff who are professional? When and how will you address those who are not?

Podcast 2.1 Words and Actions

 https://resources.corwin.com/tenminute
principal

3

RELATIONSHIP BUILDING

I n my first position as principal, I opened a junior high school. Although I was new to administration, I understood that surrounding myself with great teachers would be key to my own professional achievement and my new school's success.

The superintendent who hired me called one day in the summer and said he had a great Spanish teacher for me, a guy who attended his church. My superintendent bragged how he made a great hire for me and how I could learn from his hiring skills. Mr. McFadden, the Spanish teacher, had an Ivy League degree and recently retired from a government job. The division was able to obtain a provisional teaching license for him.

On the first day of teacher workweek, I with met new staff members. By the end of the day, I had a barrel of concerns about Mr. McFadden. My worries increased when several staff came to me at the end of the day and complained that McFadden was offensive and overly opinionated. I learned quickly that staff were spot-on. Mr. McFadden began his teaching position in August. One month later, he decided teaching was not for him, and he handed me a much-welcomed letter of resignation. As I look back, he seemed academically smart, but he had no ability to connect with students, staff, or parents. Teaching was not for him. Nor was hiring great teachers a skill of my superintendent.

Teaching and leadership are complex. The ability to build positive relationships is a common trait of effective teachers and leaders. Positive relationships alone do not make a great educator, but without the ability to make connections with others, a person can never be a great educator. We always have been, are, and always will be in the relationship business. I frequently remind myself that kids will never work their hardest for adults if they think the adults don't care about them. School staff will do their best when they feel a positive and, yes, caring connection from school leadership.

In this chapter, I'll share stories, ideas, and strategies to help you become a relationship builder who inspires others on your staff to be the same. A foundational part of being a relationship builder is making a choice each day about the kind of day you'll have, the person you are, and the educator you want to be. Choose your attitude.

ACCENTUATE THE POSITIVE, ELIMINATE THE NEGATIVE

So now for the look-in-the-mirror-moment. Ask yourself, *Am I a positive person?* Then, reflect on these statements: Positive people typically draw like-minded people to them. People who are negative often draw negative people to them. Some people believe they are positive and feel perplexed when they are surrounded by negative people. Everyone has the power to change their outlook to positive as long as each person sees the need and has the will.

> **Positive people typically draw like-minded people to them. People who are negative often draw negative people to them. Some people believe they are positive and feel perplexed when they are surrounded by negative people. #10MinutePrincipal**

After many years in education, I can honestly say that I have known quite a few negative educators, including school and district leaders. However, I have also known educators who continually maintain a positive outlook and understand that being positive is a key ingredient for success and is needed to build, foster, and sustain trusting relationships. I have never known a negative educator who has achieved success over time, but I have observed positive educators find success again and again. Positivity and negativity affect people's interactions, how they see themselves, and their view of life and the world. Choose positivity!

10-MINUTE OPPORTUNITY

Your leadership style and attitudinal choices hold the potential for creating an upbeat outlook among teachers who in turn can develop a positive class environment for students. Carry the banner of positivity and model the standard! To support your efforts, I've identified four opportunities for you to consider every day:

1. Make the personal choice to be a positive leader and influencer.
2. Be upbeat and optimistic and focus on what others do well.
3. Bring a positive outlook to negative people by modeling your brand of professionalism.
4. Practice being positive every day, all day.

10-MINUTE TIP

If the culture of your school is negative, remember this: A negative school climate and culture will inhibit a school's success. In such a school, being positive can test your leadership and at times leave you feeling lonely. To start creating a positive school culture, notice and give voice to the good you observe every day while

- completing walkthroughs;
- spending time in the cafeteria;
- walking your school's halls;

- meeting with staff and parents;
- attending school and district meetings; and
- watching sports and other extracurricular events.

Be intentional; notice and reinforce what's working well. Great school environments are not created overnight, and negative environments cannot be fixed immediately. The choices you make, relationships you create, and what you are willing to tolerate are all critical to turn an environment around.

Lead with purpose and passion; each day commit to creating a positive school culture for students and staff and parents. #10MinutePrincipal

 10-MINUTE COLLABORATION

Here are three strategies to support collaborating and communicating:

Take a Lunch Break. Lunch is a great time for the principal and staff to connect with students. Take the lead and model to staff the importance of having lunch with students, so you get to know and connect with them. In addition, you'll have an opportunity to hear ideas such as how to increase school spirit and anything else students share. When they get to know you and see you as approachable, students are more than willing to discuss their ideas.

Talk With Staff. Conversations with staff are difficult to schedule in a world that moves fast. Effective, positive

(Continued)

(Continued)

interactions will always enhance your credibility as a leader. Having conversations with staff and students is a tried and true way to achieve this goal. During informal chats, you can share your beliefs and build positive connections. When you communicate what you believe, you either draw staff to you or away from you. Either way, staff will begin to know your expectations; what you believe should always be connected to what you do and expect.

Model the Standard. Your words, actions, decisions, behaviors, and choices communicate your personal standards, your beliefs, and what you consider acceptable. If staff hear you yelling at students, you give them permission to do the same. If you're a sloppy dresser, you give permission. If you are anti-technology, you give permission. If you have low expectations for students, you give permission. If you communicate a fixed mindset, you give permission. The principal sets the tone! Model and communicate your high expectations relentlessly. Strive for congruence between what you say and what you do! If you don't have congruence, people will not pay much attention to your words—only to your actions. Every day, be an advocate and champion for learning, growth, and excellence! Every day, choose to model your standards.

BUILD COMMITMENT IN YOUR SCHOOL COMMUNITY

The best educators change pathways for students, not just in the present but also into the future. Working with students is a big responsibility and a privilege. Staff who want and give their best to their students view education as a profession, not just a job. They possess strong and developing teaching skills combined with high personal efficacy, a positive outlook, and a passion for making a difference. Encourage these kinds of teachers to become advocates for professional learning and students' needs. Teacher advocates are leaders who, with the principal's support, organize professional learning on topics their team needs, advocate for students who require additional time to improve, lobby for class libraries so students have access to books in all subjects, and support personal learning networks.

Principals who support and develop teacher advocacy among staff encourage leadership and have an ever-expanding cadre of teachers who share important responsibilities. What happens is that positive relationships between teachers and the principal develop because both groups work to improve instruction and learning by sharing and developing their expertise. When building a team, your goal should be to hire staff that have these important traits, support them, and keep them.

Every school cannot have the best teachers in America; there aren't enough to go around. You need to see potential, see talent, and be able to provide support for personal growth. Remember that the right culture and climate are always needed if your goal is to develop and retain staff. For this to happen in a school, it is important for you to know and model the traits you admire, be the standard for what a professional is in your school. Students in your school and every school deserve educators who view their work as a profession, not a job.

Address Resisters

When staff have different opinions and feel safe to share them, this can help you reflect on initiatives and specific situations.

However, when there's resistance to new ideas most of the time, you need to address this because such resistance can derail problem solving and schoolwide initiatives. No matter the number of resisters, you go wrong if you don't address resisters and work to bring them on board. Why? Because resisters often spread negative talk among staff and hold the potential of bringing many to their side. The question is *What can you do?*

TIPS ON REDUCING RESISTANCE

It's important that staff understand that you will address resistance when an initiative will positively affect learning and the school's environment. Here are some tips that can reduce resistance:

- Meet with teams and departments as well as other staff to build support for an initiative. Build consensus, but realize that having everyone on board all the time can hinder forward motion.
- Have one-on-one conversations with each resister to better understand his or her perspective and ensure yours is understood.
- Encourage conversations between resisters and staff embracing the initiative.

You'll need to find the way you address concerns, so it's a positive experience for you and the person receiving your concern. The finesse lies in the delivery. Addressing concerns is an opportunity to clarify your beliefs and expectations and help a person make positive change. Here are some situations you might meet and suggestions for dealing with them.

Pitfall: Resistance to Change. Staff who persistently resist change can derail initiatives, stifle professional learning, and limit the learning potential of students. Resisting change runs a wide gamut. It can be refusing to adopt research-based best practices, being unwilling to try collaborative learning, refusing to integrate technology, attending professional learning in body but not in mind and spirit. Beliefs and statements among staff enable you to spot resistance. Listen for comments such as, "This, too, shall pass," or "It was good enough for me, it should be good enough for these students." Some teachers have feelings of entitlement: "Families love me, so I can do what I want." Staff who resist, mock, or obstruct school goals need to change. You can choose to do nothing—remain silent when you observe acts or behaviors you don't agree with—or address them.

Try This: Extend invitations to teachers to participate in learning that can bring meaningful changes to teaching practices. Accepting an invitation means making a commitment. Have those involved in change bring artifacts and lesson results to team and department meetings and share. Enthusiasm and good news can spread like a cold. Give yourself and your staff the gift of time. Change takes time.

Pitfall: Too Much Tolerance. Beware of condoning unprofessional behaviors among staff and central office administrators in order to cultivate an alliance. If doing this is against your beliefs and values, then you will confuse staff, for they won't know what you truly stand for. Moreover, if your words and actions change with each situation, you give staff the license to do the same.

Try This: Take a deep look at yourself and have an in-the-head, reflective conversation. Make sure you understand what you believe and value and avoid compromising these beliefs. Always keep in mind your purpose—to advocate for and support children and their teachers.

Pitfall: The Countdown Mentality. In some schools, at the end of the first day you can hear staff say, "Only 179 school days left." Some teachers even keep a countdown calendar. This creates a mindset among staff that teaching is a job, not a calling and profession.

Try This: First, if you hear these comments, start a conversation immediately. Make this an expectation: Everyone is at your school to help and support children's learning and emotional well-being. Revisit this mindset at team and department meetings. Invite teachers to share how they have helped move a child forward and continually point out how the teachers' sharing illustrates why we come to work each day.

Anyone on a journey toward excellence will meet resisters along the way. But first, start with yourself and ask, *Are there beliefs and practices I need to let go of?* For change to happen in your school, you need to first look at yourself before asking others to change. Choose to let go of what's holding you back. Once you free yourself, you can work with resistance among staff.

 10-MINUTE OPPORTUNITY

Perhaps the best way to overcome resistance among staff is to continually build relationships through conversations, a positive e-mail, and noticing something great a staff member did. Once trusting relationships are in place, engaging in tough conversations is easier because the trust acts as a bridge to negotiating changes.

10-MINUTE TIP

Take ten minutes to reflect on the kinds of resistance you notice in your school, make a list, and prioritize what you'd like to tackle first, second, and so on. You can refer to my list on pages 57–58 as a reference.

10-MINUTE COLLABORATION

Maintaining a professional positive work environment is similar to watering a garden. Without water, a garden will wither. Without a focus on professionalism, it too can fade. The principal has an obligation to help staff focus and reflect on why they do what they do to keep professionalism a school focus. Look, everyone has a bad day once in a while and sits in a metaphorical hole she or he creates. The best educators may visit the hole, but they don't live in it—they refocus themselves.

Several times each year I share reflections with staff on professionalism to stretch their thinking and to bring the best instruction each day to students. These reflections can be done alone, but I encourage staff to review them in groups.

1. What if I reflect on several practices in my school or classroom that may no longer serve a purpose?

(Continued)

(Continued)

2. What if I look at my room, change the design, and make it a more interesting space for students?
3. What if the way I grade was based on best practice and research?
4. What if every day I make a choice to be positive and encouraging?
5. What if I try technology that I have not used before in my building or class?
6. What if I start using Twitter to connect to a professional learning network?
7. What if each day I model a growth mindset to my colleagues and students?
8. What if when an opportunity comes to join in, I say yes?
9. What if when I encounter negative people, I tell them to stop?
10. What if I commit to being the professional I always thought I could be?

Reflecting on these questions can lead to improved relationships with teachers and other administrators.

ADMINISTRATIVE AND TEACHER RELATIONSHIPS

I taught in the school I presently serve as principal, and after six years of teaching, I left for an administrative job in a nearby county. Five years later, I returned as principal, and many staff

I worked with as a teacher viewed me differently as principal—I was not their colleague anymore. For me, the transition was awkward, but in time and after some staff retired, the relationship piece of principal to teacher improved. I learned a few things to avoid, and I learned some ways to foster relationships. Relationships take time to build. Save some time by avoiding these pitfalls.

Pitfall: Favoritism. You're the principal, and you set the tone. Realize staff make positive or negative judgments about you based on what they see you doing or tolerating. If staff think you have favorites, you create a dynamic that is not helpful for your school climate.

Try This: You will spend many hours in your school. Make it a goal to spend time with all members of your school community and treat them the same. You set the example and have the ability to make the culture and climate better.

Pitfall: Socializing With Staff. Your job can be lonely, but socializing with staff gives them the wrong impression. Staff in your school may have groups who get together on weekends or after work. If you join in, you risk being seen by others in your school as the administrator who has favorites. This won't foster a professional climate and culture.

Try This: Be friendly to everyone but be careful when friendly changes to friendships. Being "friends" with a select group opens you up to criticism and, yet again, perceptions of favoritism.

Pitfall: Spending School Time With Select Staff. Spending time with a select group can occur without an awareness that it's happening. It can be subtle, but can send a negative message to staff observing you. Maybe there is a place you stand every morning prior to school starting, and the same staff interact with you each morning. Maybe you eat in the cafeteria the same time each day and sit with the same staff. Maybe there is one classroom you frequently stand outside of during hall changes. These behaviors can send this message to others: You have favorites.

Try This: It is natural to gravitate toward people you prefer to be around, but as a principal, this will cause challenges. Take a few minutes and think about some patterns you have during your day and whether you need to disrupt and change some. For example, if you eat lunch at the same time and same place each day, vary the time and place.

 10-MINUTE OPPORTUNITY

You work hard to build relationships and trust among staff. It's easy to ruin a trusting relationship, so it's important to guard against this. Take time to reflect on your relationships with staff, list them, and decide if some have to change. You can use my suggestions listed here or create your own list.

- Be an active listener and carefully respond to what's said.
- Notice staff's positive actions and tell them what's working.

- Have one-to-one conversations.
- Seek out collaborative opportunities with staff.
- Make sure your actions and words have a high degree of consistency.

  10-MINUTE TIP

Class walkthroughs can be a relationship builder, or they can negatively impact your school's culture and climate. When staff do not know expectations for walkthroughs, feelings of being inspected or not trusted can develop quickly. What follows are seven ways to ruin your walkthrough efforts. As you review them, do any exist in your school? If they do, how can you make a change?

1. Not building trust between teachers and administrators
2. Completing walkthroughs when staff have no clue why you're doing them
3. Never letting staff know when walkthroughs will occur
4. Inviting people not known to your staff to do walkthroughs
5. Giving no feedback to teachers afterward
6. Making a walkthrough visit evaluative
7. Huddling with other administrators outside a class where you just did a walkthrough and looking serious or angry

10-MINUTE COLLABORATION

Walkthroughs can enhance relationships and trust. They work best when there is a professional and trusting relationship between you and teachers. Consider collaborating with staff to create instructional focus areas before initiating walkthrough observations. This can bring clarity to walkthrough visits for administrators who know the purpose and for teachers who know what to expect. Establish focus areas with faculty instead of telling them, "This is what we will do." To start the process, invite teachers to look at data from the previous year, articles and books they've read on best practices in education, and instructional focus points for the upcoming school year. Then, collaborate to set three to four instructional focus areas that affect all subjects. The key is to not create too many; I suggest three to six instructional focus areas for the year. Doing this will create clarity to class walkthroughs, build trusting professional relationships, and remove the negative impact of mystery.

Here are four instructional focus areas my staff worked on:

- Engagement Versus Compliance
- Learning Targets
- Higher-Level Oral Questioning
- Effective Exit Passes

Now when you do walkthroughs, teachers know you are focusing on the "look fors" you and teachers established. Consider how you can initiate more meaningful walkthroughs in your school.

WALKTHROUGHS CAN BUILD TRUST

Marlena Gross-Taylor
Author, speaker, blogger, and founder of
#EduGladiators

As educators, we know the importance of building relationships so we might better connect with our students. The beginning of the school year is usually filled with activities to learn more about our students with team-building activities embedded throughout the school year to sustain the positive momentum.

So why does this incredible energy instantly dissipate at the mere mention of administrative walkthroughs? As an educational leader, I want to change that narrative and truly believe that if leaders apply the same concept of building relationships teachers have with students with their staff, administrators can build a trusting partnership that actually empowers teachers. Trust is essential to effective relationships, which is the foundation of developing an environment that encourages commitment over compliance to foster a culture of teamwork.

The start of a school year is hectic for administrators, but it's also a perfect opportunity to build relationships with teachers. The magic happens in the classroom, and as instructional leaders, that is exactly where administrators need to be. Walkthroughs provide the perfect platform to gain teachers' trust by being visible, engaging with students, and providing instructional feedback, which should include resources to continuously build teacher capacity.

(Continued)

(Continued)

Time is a premium for administrators, and just as teachers focus on engaging students the first couple of weeks of a new school year, so must administrators prioritize teacher relationships with walkthroughs.

Most teachers associate walkthroughs with official observations, missing the opportunity to leverage the instructional expertise of their administrators to improve their practice. However, administrators inadvertently perpetuate this anxiety by only appearing in classrooms during observations. Instead, administrators should take a cue from their teachers and focus on being visible in classroom . . . and without the laptop, iPad, walkie-talkie, and notebook in tow.

At the start of each school year, I intentionally block off a minimum of two hours in my calendar to visit classrooms for at least minutes, using a checklist of all teachers to ensure I walk through each classroom at least twice over the first few weeks of school. Unless the school is on fire, my front office staff helps me protect this time by limiting disruptions.

When I walk into a classroom, the students usually ask if I am there to observe the teacher (yes, they know the observation routine well) and are usually surprised when I share that my office is boring and I want to have fun learning with them. The teacher is at ease because I am without the usual observation tools mentioned earlier, and the students become accustomed to my presence. After my first visit, I write a handwritten note to the teachers, thanking them for allowing me to participate in their classrooms, how excited I am to have them on staff, and if there is anything they might need. Feedback after the second visit is a quick e-mail specifying a positive I observed and a suggestion or question to open the lines of honest communication.

Timely feedback is critical to easing teacher anxiety and should always be given when an administrator visits a classroom, focusing on the positive to address any instructional areas of refinement. I also encourage peer walkthroughs based on our school instructional priorities to develop a culture of continuous improvement built on trust between teachers. Walkthroughs are a powerful practice to improve instruction and transform the learning experiences of our students.

DISRUPTING ROUTINES

All of us have our own feelings about change. There will be times when you and staff embrace change and feel liberated. Other times, change can be uncomfortable or scary. Sometimes in education we do things for no real reason other than we have always done it that way. Sometimes our thinking alone holds us back. Disrupting routines, patterns, and traditions can support positive change in your school.

Every reader of this book has something in common: We all have gone through school. Our experiences and beliefs often shape how we view school. However, such experiences can be harmful if they influence how we approach leadership or educating students.

To jump-start your thinking, I am sharing a list of practices that staff and I have collaborated on to create change. Some of the practices may even bring back fond memories, but this does not mean they are good for today's students.

CREATE CHANGE BY QUESTIONING
COMMON PRACTICES

1. **How We Grade**. Grading is a challenging conversation to have. Fortunately, there is a lot of research on best practice and how grading can inform what a student knows compared to the curriculum. Few teachers come out of school with a deep understanding of best grading practices. To be honest, when I was a teacher I graded based on my recollections of how my favorite teachers graded me. In some instances, this was fine; others, not fine at all. Use of zeroes, averaging, total point systems, failure, and using grades to punish are a few not-so-fine methods that come to mind. Even though it can create discomfort among staff, grading topics should be discussed and compared to current research.

2. **Extra Credit.** Bringing a box of tissues to class is a nice thing to do, but counting it as a test grade will create an inaccuracy about a student's knowledge of the curriculum. Grades should reflect what students have mastered and should not be influenced by extra credit. Most readers grew up with extra credit, and many parents will ask for ways to earn extra credit. This does not mean extra credit should continue.

3. **Notebook Checks for Grades**. Do students need to learn how to organize for class and school? Absolutely! Notebook checks can be valuable, but it's OK if they aren't graded. An organized notebook communicates very little about a student's knowledge of the curriculum. Moreover, everything a teacher assesses does not need to be recorded in a grade book.

4. **Planning for the Year.** Great teachers plan and have larger outlines of where their curriculum is going over the course of the year. But each class is different. Well-designed formative assessment can serve as an indicator for which groups can move forward and which need reteaching. Formative assessments help teachers plan. It makes no sense to plan ahead for the entire year because such planning doesn't use student learning as a guide. This type of rigidity can be harmful and often allows a staff member to say, "I taught it; they didn't learn it."

10-MINUTE OPPORTUNITY

I would like to challenge you to think differently and reflect on your relationship with practices and traditions that may be in place in your school but may require change. Start by reflecting on your school and generate a list of practices you believe may need to change. Collaborate with staff and discuss, set priorities, and plan a course of action.

10-MINUTE TIP

Possibly some of my change areas resonate with you or maybe you have some different ideas. My examples and the practices you likely listed often range from relatively

(Continued)

(Continued)

quick adjusts to yearlong study. Some may seem quick, but when you dig deeper, they are not. For example, extra credit has lived in schools and in family conversations for many years. Without a doubt, there are staff and families who value it and see no harm. Certainly, there are many parents who have fond memories of extra credit when they were students. Changing how extra credit is given (or not) can be a challenge; it needs to happen, but it does not need to be the first hurdle you cross. Consider starting with a practice held less dear, one you believe needs attention in your school and also provides a quick win. I chose notebook checks for grades.

After choosing the practice, you have two options. The first option, which I do not recommend, is to declare a ban on the practice. Top-down decisions do not create buy-in; avoid them as much as possible. The second option is to start a discussion on the topic by sharing with staff one or several thought-provoking articles easily read in ten minutes. Do not be judgmental; share a view different from the practice you observed. Here is a simple format to get the process going: Pose a statement, ask a question, and set a follow-up opportunity.

Statement: This article made me think in new ways about a practice we've had in place for some time.

Pose a Question: Please read the article. What does the author suggest we do different?

Follow-Up Opportunity: I will be coming to your grade-level meeting on Wednesday to hear your thoughts, ideas, and suggestions. I look forward to our discussion.

10-MINUTE COLLABORATION

Some practices that need attention are complex and can take a year or more to bring substantive change. If you are going to take a full school year to learn and create a pathway to change, where you spend your time is important. Extra credit may be tricky to navigate, but spending a year studying it makes little sense. On the other hand, grading practices or how a school's schedule could be different are solid choices for a yearlong study. Let's further explore how grading could be an ongoing topic for staff study.

At times, a representative committee of staff members makes sense. But when your school is exploring potentially significant changes to practice, you can't create positive change by only working with a representative committee. My suggestion will slow the process down, but it is better for teachers to be involved through faculty meeting study groups. Consider setting aside fifteen minutes of each faculty meeting to brainstorm ideas or discuss questions and comments on a shared article. By the middle of the year, an action committee of select teachers can be nominated from peers to move the process along at a quicker pace. But this should only happen after staff have had an opportunity to work collectively and engage in discussions.

EXPECTATIONS AND SPECIFIC PRAISE

Giving specific praise and communicating expectations to students and staff is an important skill and practice. Both specific praise and clear expectations can provide the feedback needed for personal and professional growth and professional relationships. The caveat is that praise needs to be genuine and expectations clear.

I recall a time when my school division was absorbed in the belief that all students and staff needed to be told they were unique and valuable all the time. My principal enthusiastically modeled and encouraged staff to tell each other and students they were unique and valuable, and it was done constantly. She would walk up to a teacher, look at the teacher with some conviction and say, "You're unique and valuable." It still makes me cringe. Very quickly the slogan "You're unique and valuable" became a joke. First, it was made fun of quietly, but the subtlety faded quickly, and staff mocked it openly. Why? Because the saying meant nothing, and there were no specifics behind the words. It was a poorly imagined school venture. Specific praise and clear expectations are essential for professional growth.

 10-MINUTE OPPORTUNITY

When communicating expectations, consider how staff receive and react to them. Are expectations in writing, are they orally communicated, and most importantly, are they stated positively? Schools have a wide range of expectations, from when staff arrive and leave work to instructional and professional expectations. If you have not already done so, add expectations to your faculty handbook and revisit them throughout the year. Expectations are fine if communicated positively; if not, they hurt relationships, school climate, and culture. Here are examples of a positively stated and poorly stated expectation:

Positive: Please arrive to work by 7:45 so you can check mail and be prepared for a great day with students.

Negative: Staff who are not in the building by 7:45 will receive one verbal warning; upon the second offense, a letter will be written documenting lateness and placed in the staff member's personnel file.

Take time and review expectations in your faculty handbook and any other expectations you communicate in writing. This will ensure that staff perceives each one as upbeat and fair.

> **Positional authority may give a person the power to make people do things, but positional authority does not have the power to make people care. #10MinutePrincipal**

10-MINUTE TIP

The nonspecific, feel-good praise my principal adopted was a failure. People need to hear more than a shallow, "You're unique and valuable." However, praise works quite well when it's specific. It's easy to overuse certain positive phrases because you feel good saying them and

(Continued)

(Continued)

often receive a smile in return. Sayings such as, "You're awesome" or "You're the smartest/best/nicest" aren't bad—they just lack specificity.

Each year at our opening faculty meeting, staff study nonspecific praise and discuss how to make each one specific. At times in my career, I assumed that staff used specific praise and my administrative team modeled it. It was inconsistent. The praise teachers and administrators delivered improved because we revisited it several times during the year.

What we prioritize gets done. #10MinutePrincipal

 10-MINUTE COLLABORATION

Specific praise is not just for administrators and teachers; it is a great skill to teach students. Through your student advisory team or student government, promote specific praise. Explain and teach students the difference between vague praise and specific praise. I have used examples such as the following:

- You're a great friend because . . .
- You're a great band member because . . .
- You're a great athlete because . . .
- You're a great student because . . .
- You're a great teacher because . . .

This will get a conversation going, but you will need to gently guide students toward use of specific words. "You're a good friend because you're nice" is not specific.

Positive Praise Post-its is a good activity for students to further promote specific praise. Each day for a week, fill colorful sticky notes with positive praise and kind words; then, place several on student lockers or on classroom doors. Something so simple can have a great ripple effect across a school to promote a positive environment and the use of specific praise. Give it a try!

TELL YOUR STORY

The connections between members of a school community will always be part of what makes a school successful. Relationships with parents and your community are part of a school's success. Social media can serve as a bridge to better connect your school with parents and your community, as well as strengthen relationships. Eric Sheninger, in his 2017 book *BrandED,* notes that you need to be the storyteller-in-chief for your school. Eric also reminds us that we need to tell our story or someone else will. Using social media allows a school to communicate information quickly to students, parents, and your community. Facebook, video, Twitter, and Instagram are free, allowing you and your staff to inform and celebrate all that occurs in your school. Communicating and informing in positive ways impact how people view your school, which impacts climate and culture. Never underestimate the power of story—tell yours!

**10-MINUTE REFLECTIONS
ON OPPORTUNITIES FOR
CHANGE**

Trusting and positive relationships are part of effective schools. What changes do you need to make right now to improve your relationships with parents, staff, and students?

- How do you model and promote the importance of professionalism?
- Are you a positive person? Remember, this is a choice.
- How can you better model positivity to parents, staff, and students?
- How can you help others see the value of positive relationships? What will your first step be?

Podcast 3.1 Accentuate the Positive

 https://resources.corwin.com/tenminute principal

4

PURPOSEFUL MEETINGS

T ime is valuable. Every day ask yourself this question: *Am I using my time in the most effective ways for my staff, my students, and myself?* Time can easily be swallowed up by parts of your job that may not have an impact on teaching and learning. For example, spending several hours a day in the cafeteria may increase visibility, but is it truly the best use of time? Meetings should always use time effectively and efficiently; otherwise, those attending fail to see their value. During my teaching career, I've experienced effective and ineffective meetings.

When I was a third-year teacher we had weekly faculty meetings after school for up to two hours. Frequently, these were two painful hours for me and others. Our typical discussion topics: how to curtail gum chewing, students who wear hats, and general dress code violations. There is one truly ineffective meeting I recall vividly: a lengthy discussion of what type of sodas would be in the vending machine. During the meeting, a veteran staff member delivered an impassioned speech on her love of orange soda and why it should have a place in our soda machine. Consensus is good, but much of what we discussed was simply not important. As I reflect on my experience from the "soda" faculty meeting, I realize that meeting and many others lacked alignment with what our school was really trying to accomplish. Oddly enough, we didn't spend much time discussing teaching and learning. It was meeting for the sake of meeting. Such meetings have little value, and based on my experience, staff quickly resent them.

Teaching and learning should always be a priority for school meetings throughout the year. To hone the discussion, I suggest working with staff to create a few key initiatives for the school year, and these initiatives should focus on teaching and learning.

FOCUS INITIATIVES ON TEACHING AND LEARNING

School initiatives should be limited to three to four carefully chosen focus areas for your school, known by all staff. Notice I said three to four. Many schools experience initiative overload; too many initiatives benefit no one at all. Each year through feedback, observation, conversation, and data, you can put forth three or four school initiatives and bring focus to your school and school meetings.

Initiatives should be broad and connect to all staff through professional development, a book study, article shares, and social media. For example, writing across the curriculum can be a school-wide initiative; it's applicable to every subject. On the other hand, capitalization rules are not a yearlong initiative. I am not saying capitalization is unimportant, but it's not a schoolwide focus for substantive change to a writing program. When considering initiatives, decide whether they can be applicable to all subjects. Staff need to know your school initiatives, and you need to infuse them into your school, including meetings. Consider the positive impact of staff knowing the school initiatives and refining them over the entire school year. Here are three initiatives I have used in my school:

- Innovation
- Blended learning
- The changing roles of student and teacher

Initiatives can add purpose and focus to your school.

CREATING EFFECTIVE AGENDAS AND EFFECTIVE MEETINGS

Meetings are a fact of life in all schools, and organized agendas increase the likelihood of having well-run meetings. You can make meetings purposeful by integrating schoolwide initiatives. I'll share stories and strategies to design and lead effective meetings in concert with school initiatives.

What follow are examples designed to help you effectively lead a variety of meetings, including full faculty, administrative, team, and department. In addition, intentional agendas have clear purposes and result in meetings that support teaching and learning.

10-MINUTE OPPORTUNITY

Take ten minutes to reflect on the practice of your present school. Consider these three simple but telling questions:

- Are agendas created for meetings in your school?
- Can you access a record of meetings in a staff calendar?
- When appropriate, are meeting minutes sent to staff?

Meeting agendas should not be long. Be specific when developing an agenda and prioritize what's important. Adding your school initiatives to meeting agendas keeps them a point of focus and allows for meaningful conversations, updates, and staff sharing positive actions.

It is always good to seek feedback about initiatives, share successes, or to seek assistance if frustrated. What is prioritized gets done. #10MinutePrincipal

10-MINUTE TIP

You and I both know most adults can tell if a person leading a meeting is winging it. Use Google Docs to create meeting agendas! Plan ahead and consider sending out a framework agenda in a shared document two days prior to a meeting. This provides staff with an opportunity to review the agenda and add suggestions. Frame up the agenda and share it with the staff who will attend the meeting. Include what you wish to discuss but also allow staff to participate by adding to the agenda. And, of course, add your school initiatives!

SAMPLE AGENDA

At the end of the meeting, we will debrief and share how today's meeting supports our initiatives.

Date:

Topics

- Response to intervention
- Data analysis of universal screening
- Tier 1 instruction discussion
- Goal review for Tier 2 and 3 students
- Math
- English
- Tier adjustment
- Other: Add any additional items you would like to discuss.

School Initiatives

- Innovation
- Blended learning
- The changing role of student and teacher

10-MINUTE COLLABORATION

Delegate and share. When appropriate, collaborative agendas and meetings send a positive message to staff. My experience is that most staff want the opportunity to

(Continued)

(Continued)

participate collaboratively instead of being told what to do. Seeking input from your colleagues demonstrates your willingness to consider their ideas. If you do it all, staff can see this as the "boss mentality." Trust me, staff won't like it. Relationships are a pillar of school and teacher leadership; seeking input tells staff you value their ideas, and doing this improves relationships with you. If you want to explore collaborative agendas, seek input several days prior to the meeting. Asking staff for ideas the day of the meeting or at the start of the meeting is, in my opinion, not good practice.

 10-MINUTE TIP

How do staff in your school know what occurred in key building meetings? The solution is simple: Take and communicate minutes of meetings. You can take minutes during the meeting or appoint someone to take them. If you appoint someone, I suggest reviewing minutes prior to e-mailing them to staff. Be consistent. Send minutes to staff for meetings and allow staff to be in the know. Keeping informed and focused is part of creating a healthy school culture. You don't want staff to wonder about topics or results of discussions; inform them.

TEACHING-CENTERED FACULTY MEETINGS

I have experienced plenty of traditional faculty meetings. In traditional meetings, the principal often stands in front of the faculty, at times with a legal pad to read off dictums. It is time for this type of meeting to stop.

When I was a new principal, organizing and leading faculty meetings caused me great stress. I was not sure how to "do" meetings differently than the ways I experienced them as a teacher. My school had a tradition of one faculty meeting per month. As the meeting got closer, I felt mounting pressure to disseminate information and appear in charge. I was way off base with how to lead faculty meetings; I want you to avoid the errors I made.

- Think differently. Faculty meetings should mirror the student-centered learning we expect in the classroom. Reflect on what a teacher-centered faculty meeting might look like.
- Flip the script. Instead of disseminating information during meetings, e-mail announcements to teachers a few days prior to the meeting. Having teachers doing the work, not the principal, will support their efforts in redefining the teacher–student role in a classroom.
- Gain support for this change by visiting team meetings to discuss the rationale behind the new faculty meeting format. Encourage teachers to offer suggestions.
- Based on feedback I received from my staff, I organized teachers into groups and let them choose an article related to one of the topics they had suggested. Teachers read, discussed, and wrote about their reading, then shared key points with everyone in ways that bolstered their efforts to integrate twenty-first century skills into lessons.

- Many schools communicate a desire to enhance curriculum with twenty-first century skills: collaboration, communication, critical thinking, and creativity in classrooms. Think of faculty meetings as an opportunity for you to model modern skills and the collaborative learning you expect to see in classrooms.

It is disingenuous to conduct meetings where you expect staff to sit as compliant learners while you speak of collaborative classrooms. A faculty meeting should model what you expect in a classroom. #10MinutePrincipal

 10-MINUTE OPPORTUNITY

Staff will appreciate the opportunity to provide feedback and will offer it as long as there are no reprisals. Ask your staff, *What do you like about faculty meetings in their current form?* This can be done through casual conversations or a Google form. If you sense that staff feel uncomfortable to share, then make the Google form anonymous.

When I do this, I get some excellent suggestions that also reveal an understanding of staff's perceptions. For example, I discovered these interests among staff by just asking them to inform me. Staff was interested in learning more about the following:

- Research-based grading practices
- Before, during, and after learning strategies
- Differentiating instruction
- Project-based learning

When you ask for feedback, you need to accept the good and the bad. There are times when the feedback you receive is not what you expected. Make these opportunities positive, allowing you to demonstrate how all feedback can create a path for improvement.

Here are two simple questions your staff can easily answer in ten minutes. Remind them to offer specific examples:

- What do you like about our faculty meetings?
- What changes would make our meetings better?

Based on my experience, administrators rarely ask these simple questions. Ask them and encourage staff to respond honestly. Now, take a few minutes to reflect on what this tells staff about you. Hopefully, they will understand that you value their feedback and can listen to diverse views, even if these differ from yours.

 ## 10-MINUTE TIP

Let's shake things up and present a very different type of meeting. I am sharing with you a memo I sent to staff in preparation for this meeting. As you review my message to staff, consider if this or something similar can work in your school.

Memo to Staff

In order to increase the efficiency and change the dynamic of our January meeting, please have the following

(*Continued*)

(Continued)

reviewed and completed prior to our faculty meeting on January 2:

- Please list five topics you believe are important for us to focus on as a faculty. Consider our three school initiatives when suggesting topics and make sure that what you list are applicable across disciplines. Some examples could be team building, remediation, communication, teaching strategies, technology integration, homework, grading, or conducting a parent meeting. By no means is this an exclusive list. Create your list of five items and rank them from most to least important.
- On January 2, we will break into groups; staff will share their lists. The goal will be for the faculty to collectively review ideas, find commonalities, and then come to consensus on the top five items in rank order. Our top five will be topics for the last five faculty meetings this year.

We have several options for how to lead meetings and discussions during our remaining faculty meetings. Please choose the option you prefer. This will be tallied in groups on January 2, and majority will rule.

1. Topics assigned to teams
2. Topics assigned to departments
3. Topics assigned to groups made of members across disciplines and grade level

Take ten minutes to consider the message the memo sends about collaboration, consensus, communication, and inclusive leadership. How can this or something similar work in your school?

10-MINUTE COLLABORATION

Encourage staff to collaborate and share practices in their classroom that support your school's initiatives. This can be part of every faculty meeting, and it's a positive way to begin or bring closure to a meeting. At each meeting, set aside ten to fifteen minutes for several staff to share a success story about school initiatives. Model what you want! Initiative sharing offers staff the opportunity to discuss and then demonstrate practices others can use in their classrooms—all in support of the school's key initiatives.

For example, blended learning is an initiative in my school. While walking around the school, I noticed a science and math teacher effectively using the Think-Tac-Toe strategy to create differentiated opportunities for students. Normally, these teachers would not have much opportunity to collaborate. Connecting them through the strategy, which was one of our school initiatives, proved to be a great experience. Both presented at a faculty meeting, and I reinforced how the strategy supported our school initiative. Equally important, their presentation gave others ideas on how to use the strategy.

MEETINGS WITH ADMINISTRATIVE STAFF

The pace of school days can be fast. Setting time to meet with your administrative team, assistant principals, and other administrators can be hard to find, but it is important to do. During my first few years as a principal, I did not reserve time to meet with my administrative team. I assumed we were on the same page. I was dead wrong. It doesn't matter whether your school is large or small—meeting on a set schedule is important.

 10-MINUTE OPPORTUNITY

Take ten minutes, review your calendar, and schedule a weekly meeting with your administrative team for the entire year. If you don't schedule these meetings in advance, they usually stop happening. The start of the year is the best time to note meetings on your calendar. However, you can do it anytime; just start from where you are and schedule out the year. I suggest you consider 9:00 a.m. meetings because by this time, students and teachers are in class.

 10-MINUTE TIP

Ten minutes is all you need to craft an agenda, share it with your team, and invite them to add additional items. Agendas should be sent two days prior to the meeting. Minutes should be taken so you and your administrative team have a record of the discussion topics. Finally, I suggest rotating among team members for taking minutes.

10-MINUTE COLLABORATION

Being on the same page about how your school is led and managed is important, and it happens when you and your administrative team communicate and collaborate. Prioritize the meeting by addressing the pressing issues first, then follow up with next-step items and school initiatives. This allows you to discuss and problem solve while not losing sight of the larger picture of where your school is going. When there's limited time, it can be tempting to miss an opportunity to discuss progress toward your building's initiatives. Don't!

For example, innovation is an initiative in my school. During meetings, my administrative team and I discuss how we are innovating. Since social media is important in my school, in meetings I frequently ask this question: *How are you using our school's social media to spread the message about the positive things happening in our school?* Remember, what you communicate as important needs to become a priority among your administrative team, so all of you transmit the same message.

TEAM AND DEPARTMENT MEETINGS

Continual communication impacts your school's operation. Your message should always express how much you value keeping staff in the loop about what's happening in the school. Organized team and department meetings provide opportunities for teacher leadership and advocacy. These meetings can offer members opportunities to make recommendations affecting curriculum, professional learning, and students' needs.

10-MINUTE OPPORTUNITY

The lead grade-level teacher or department chair is in charge of their meetings. Meeting norms and expectations help make meetings more effective, but don't presume they are in place. If you are new to a school, ask a grade-level or department leader if meeting norms and expectations are in place and what they are. If norms and expectations are not in place, take ten minutes to share some general ideas and consider additional contributions teachers might want to add to their meetings. Keep your expectations simple and clear.

Meeting Norms and Expectations

- Schedule meetings for the year.
- Share an agenda with team/department members two days prior to the meeting.
- Take and share minutes with team members and administration.
- Discuss school initiatives at each meeting.
- Make sure everyone's voice is heard.
- Balance your participation and listen more than you speak.
- Listen actively and respond to what team members say.

10-MINUTE TIP

Communicate to your team and department leaders your willingness to attend meetings as long as an invitation has been sent to you. Staff needs time to work together and feel you trust them. Attending every meeting potentially inhibits honest conversation and gives the impression you don't trust teachers to work independently of you. Relationships are based on trust. Be trusting until you have reason not to be. Staff will appreciate your trust in them.

10-MINUTE COLLABORATION

Meet with grade-level leaders and department chairs through leadership meetings. Consider meeting once a week with all grade-level leaders and once or twice per month with all department chairs. Your calendar can fill up quickly. Therefore, I suggest scheduling these meetings for the entire school year. Each meeting should follow your established school norms and expectations.

Consider my school's schedule for these meetings. I meet after school with grade-level leaders each Monday and department chairs the third Thursday of each month. In addition to discussing school-based items, these standing meetings are yet another opportunity to focus for ten minutes on your school's initiatives through discussion and by sharing successes and challenges. By now, you've noticed there is a repetition of formally inserting the school initiatives in meetings. This strategy will ensure that initiatives are not forgotten and remain a focus throughout the year.

As you read on, you'll explore meetings that address instruction and parent meetings that can be positive or confrontational. Postobservation meetings allow you to support best practices and offer suggestions for improving teaching and learning. Meeting with parents provides opportunities to help them understand how they can support their children. These meetings also enable you to deepen parents' knowledge of your school's mission and initiatives.

POSTOBSERVATION MEETINGS

Postobservation meetings should occur the same day as your class observation. This can be challenging, but it's an excellent goal to set. Feedback is critical for growth, and to be effective, it must be timely. Delaying feedback for several days or up to a week weakens the conversation and its value to the teacher. Consider this coaching example: I am your basketball coach, and you are practicing free throws from the line. If your form is off, I'm going to stop you, give you feedback, or demonstrate the correct form. Then, I'll have you try again and provide specific, positive feedback. What I would *not* do is watch your form, note what needs to change, and discuss it with you several days later. Good coaches provide timely feedback. Effective principals do the same.

Good coaches provide timely feedback. Effective principals do much the same. #10MinutePrincipal

 10-MINUTE OPPORTUNITY

Take ten minutes to reflect on the timeliness of your post-observation feedback. It is important to reflect on your practice to consider if there are changes to make. Here are three simple questions to consider:

- Is a same-day postobservation conversation an expectation you have for yourself and your administrative team?
- How are you communicating expectations?
- Are teachers provided questions for reflection to guide postobservation discussion?

Here are two common and not-so-good postobservation questions:

- ✗ What do you think went well with the observed lesson?
- ✗ What would you do differently when teaching this lesson again?

10-MINUTE TIP

In order to have a substantive postobservation discussion, provide teachers with reflective questions about their lesson to guide the postevaluation conversation. My questions are probing and designed to elicit thinking.

Postobservation Reflection Questions

- How did you generate interest in the lesson?
- How engaged were the students? How do you know students were engaged?
- Who did the instruction work for? Who didn't it work for? How do you know?

(Continued)

(Continued)

- What were some strategies you used to enhance learning? How did these strategies enhance the learning of your students?
- What strategies could you have used to better enhance learning?
- What were some after-learning activities you used?
- How might you better prompt students to reflect on what they learned?
- Why did you design the sequence of activities the way you did to meet your lesson objectives?
- How could you design the lesson differently to further evidence learning?
- How does your lesson support our three school initiatives?
- Now that your lesson is complete, what will you teach this group of students the next time you have class with them? How have you determined this is the next step? What evidence did you collect from your students that led you to this decision? What will you do for those it did not work for?

I review my postobservation questions at a faculty meeting early in the year by carefully reviewing the what, how, and why. Teachers receive three questions from my list prior to my observation.

I suggest that staff write down some notes for each question instead of writing them out. In the past when I have not directly asked for notes to be taken, some staff have been unprepared. During a postobservation meeting, I open by inviting the teacher to review his or her notes for the three selected questions. I listen without interrupting, and this is important because I want to honor and respect their responses and listen to all of them so I can better respond and ask questions. A typical teacher response is that the lesson worked for the class. That's when I probe deeper with questions such as, *Did every student understand the lesson? Were there students who couldn't do the work? Were there students who found the work easy?* These questions moved us into a discussion of differentiating and how the teacher could make such adjustments.

10-MINUTE COLLABORATION

Practice how to do a postobservation conference with your administrative team. Reach out to an effective teacher on your team and let the person know you would like to practice a debrief, using the questions with them and a member of your administrative team. This is a great coaching opportunity for an assistant principal and also beneficial for the teacher. In addition, the teacher can follow up with other teachers to better explain the postobservation process.

MENTORING SESSIONS

Mentorship is needed for professionals to grow. An effectively organized and coordinated mentor program can not only increase teacher effectiveness, but it also can reduce turnover.

To this day, I can recall my first job as a history teacher. I was new to the profession; it was the first day of new-teacher workweek. Diligently, I was organizing my desk when a teacher knocked on my door. I welcomed her in; she said she could only stay a few minutes. She then presented me with several work-books and a teacher's edition of the textbook I was to use. She was the department chair. I still recall the exact words she shared with me: "Well, Evan, I typically make it to Chapter 23 each year; you try to do the same." Shortly after, she left. During my first year, we had two department meetings, and no person in the school ever helped me. It was sink or swim—truly a horrible way to start a teaching career.

MENTORSHIP

Dr. Nathan Lang-Raad
Speaker, consultant, and author of *Everyday Instructional Coaching: Seven Daily Drivers to Support Teacher Effectiveness* (2018)

We are at a crossroads in education where the role of the teacher is changing dramatically. The role has been chang-ing the past two decades, to a student-centric classroom. This does not mean the teacher role is diminished—actually, quite the opposite. It's never been so important. In any classroom, the most successful learning occurs when the teacher is a facilitator or activator of learning. Furthermore, successful teaching occurs when principals, coaches, and fellow teachers are effective mentors and activators of pro-fessional learning. We expect teachers to shift from drills, worksheets, and rote memorization to designing learning experiences that build on student strengths and experi-ences. Should professional learning be the same, where we expect school leaders to support teacher professional growth through meaningful job-embedded experiences? Where teachers are empowered to create new ways of teaching and model the kind of problem solving and perseverance we expect from students? To better support teachers in this shift of practice, we must provide coaching and mentorship that supports risk-taking, creativity, and innovation. Mentorship doesn't inherently happen within a leadership role. There must be clearly defined structures to ensure both the mentor and mentee get the most out of mentorship.

At the onset, it's important that the mentor and mentee communicate what they want to see happen as a result of the coaching relationship. Establishing and communicating clear norms and goals with the mentee will set the tone for positive interactions and aspirations.

The process of co-creating learning goals between the coach and teacher addresses any anxiety or misconceptions that the mentee may have about the mentor or about coaching. The most successful mentor–mentee (coach–teacher) relationships are ones built on safety, trust, and respect and when both understand and share each other's vision for professional success.

Another important aspect in establishing procedures is to provide a structure and frequency for communication and feedback. In the past, coaches and leaders might communicate through e-mail or an observation form. But everyday, friendly, and specific feedback to teachers will be more helpful than formal communication that feels bureaucratic and ungenuine.

(Continued)

(Continued)

Frey and Fisher (2011) explain that feedback in the classroom must be timely, understandable, and actionable. The concept is applied within the mentor–mentee relationship. This ensures teachers have time to act and implement the feedback through revision. The specific or understandable nature of feedback ensures teachers know exactly what parts of their practice could be strengthened and how it could be strengthened. Actionable feedback ensures teachers can take an objective view of the mentor feedback and immediately make changes. It is important that language isn't vague or centered around praising a teacher for "a great lesson" or "dynamic presentation." Affirmation is an important but separate aspect of feedback.

If working in an online collaborative document, will the mentor provide comments in the document itself? Or in a face-to-face conference? These structures should be established and explicitly communicated.

Finally, make it clear that responsibility is a very important principle to the teaching profession. Mentors and mentees must both agree that this is nonnegotiable. Teachers are responsible for their own learning, with mentors and leaders creating the best conditions for learning with ample resources and support. If a teacher produces work that doesn't meet expectations, it's the responsibility of the coach and the teacher to determine why it doesn't meet expectations (as measured by previously communicated goals) and determine how they could strengthen the work in order meet or exceed expectations. Responsible behaviors include coming to meetings on time, ending on time, preparing for meetings ahead of time, and respecting each other's opinions. Mentor responsibility involves making sure that the teacher feels valued in the school building and the community.

We should view mentorship as a powerful support system to help teachers and students think, learn, collaborate, and create in new and previously unimagined ways. Consequently, this support begins to influence a teacher's belief system about his or her own practice, with a change in behaviors following suit. When the school leader clearly articulates his or her mission and leads in accordance with that mission daily, coaching and mentoring can begin to deliver on the promise of being a game changer in education.

 10-MINUTE OPPORTUNITY

Some mentor programs are very organized with one or several staff members assigned to lead the program; this is more common in larger divisions. Smaller divisions can have no mentoring programs, an informal program, or a program in which mentoring is an additional part of a teacher's job—not ideal, but budgets and personnel can be limited in smaller divisions.

Take ten minutes to develop an understanding of your mentor program. A quick assessment of your division's programs will either be affirming or reveal some opportunities for change. Use these questions and statements for a quick assessment:

- Does my division have a formalized mentor program, or is it informal and based on building-level decisions?

(*Continued*)

(Continued)

Teachers deserve a formalized program. If one does not exist, starting a mentorship program may be dependent on the principal. Even with the best intentions, it can be challenging to single-handedly coordinate a mentor program.

- Are new teachers in your division assigned a mentor, and do mentor teachers have training to be effective mentors?

Effective mentorship is a skill, and it is best for a division to have a coordinated mentor training program. If no training is in place, consider doing a book study or article study about mentoring with teachers considering this role.

- Is there a formalized schedule for mentors and mentees to meet, and does your division have new-teacher meetings scheduled over the course of the school year?

Without formally scheduled and organized meetings, there is a high likelihood that meetings will diminish and fade away over time.

 10-MINUTE TIP

Who should you choose to be a mentor? Whether it is your own school program or your division program, who you choose as mentors is important, and it speaks to what you value. Make sure mentors you choose are a good fit with new hires. Avoid choosing based on seniority because this doesn't always mean the teacher has the necessary skills. Instead, choose your best teachers, those aligned with the vision and direction of your school. For example, if innovative instruction and effective tech integration are important for your school, choose a mentor who exemplifies these traits. In addition, consider personality when connecting mentors with mentees.

10-MINUTE COLLABORATION

Encourage peer observation in your school (see Figure 4.1). Effective peer observation helps teachers grow. Communicate a framework for peer observation or effectiveness will wane. "How was the class?" Response: "It was great." Many staff can be uncomfortable providing feedback to each other, often because they don't want to hurt a colleague's feelings. One way to front-load a peer observation initiative is to share reflective questions with staff to use during a follow-up conversation. This can be done in a faculty meeting where you explain the purpose of peer observation and review your framework with teachers.

I always let staff know this is a teacher-to-teacher growth opportunity, and I do not want anyone reporting back to me. This simple statement demonstrates trust, a pillar of effective leadership.

Figure 4.1   **Peer Observation "Look Fors" and Conversation Starters**

Grouping	Instructional Planning, Organization, and Delivery	Student Engagement and Motivation
Students are in challenging curriculum based on data from the preassessment.	The teacher is clear about learning targets and objectives.	Students have multiple options at an appropriate level from which to choose.
When a student can do an assigned task, the student is able to move immediately to a more appropriate task.	The teacher uses grouping appropriately based on instructional needs and students' readiness and interests.	Students understand the goals of the class and their shared responsibility in academic growth.
Desk arrangement depends on the instruction in the classroom.	The teacher integrates before, during, and after learning strategies.	Students recognize required and suggested tasks as respectful, authentic, and worthy of time and effort.
Grouping is flexible, based on the needs of students. Groups change based on assessments that show learning.	Teachers demonstrate clearly that individual growth is central to success in the classroom.	Students engage in meaningful learning activities relevant to their lives.

STUDENT MEETINGS

When I was in high school, I didn't even know who my principal was. Take time to meet with students. Connecting with them should always be a priority because it builds relationships and helps students bond to you and their school. There is an old saying that kids won't work for you until they know you care for them. Of course, the same is true for adults. You have many opportunities to connect in a positive way with students by saying hello, by giving a high-five, and by chatting in the hallways. These connections contribute to a positive school environment and help define culture. Effective school leaders know the value of teacher–student relationships, and they demonstrate the commitment by modeling relationship building with students, teachers, and parents. But let's think about more formalized ways for you to connect, listen, and hear students' voices.

10-MINUTE OPPORTUNITY

Do a quick check of the structures in your school for you to connect with students. Here are some questions to guide you:

- Have you created a principal–student advisory group?
- Does your school have an active student government with set meetings for you to attend?
- Are you meeting with student athletic teams, the arts, or clubs?
- Are you connecting to students through your guidance department?

As you reflect on my questions, consider which one is your top priority. All four can and should exist in any school. If these are missing, make a commitment for change but don't try to do it instantly. Change takes time. Pick the most pressing issue and start there.

10-MINUTE TIP

Set up a principal–student advisory council. If you are in an elementary or middle school, partner with teachers to define the characteristics of students for this leadership opportunity. For a school with grade-level teams, discuss the initiative with teachers and ask the team leader to submit two to four names to you for each grade level. These students can serve as your advisory council. I suggest you meet once a month to receive feedback from students and actively listen to their ideas and challenges.

For high school, consider an application form with a description of skills you are looking for. Also include an explanation of the time commitment, your goals, and the schedule for monthly after-school meetings, including their start time. Advisory groups are a great way to gauge the pulse of your school from students' perspectives.

10-MINUTE COLLABORATION

I attended a small private school from first to eighth grade. Ninth grade was my first experience in a public school, and I knew very few students. For me, and I am sure many others, starting a new school and not knowing other students was intimidating and scary. The school I attended did not have a practice in place for staff to connect with new students and ease their transition to the school. And, of course, this made adjusting hard.

Students want to feel connected. I encourage you to explore additional ways for increasing students' connections to your school. Make students new to your school a priority. Team up with your guidance staff to host new-student lunches at the start of the school year. This lunch should be for students new to your school no matter what grade level they are entering. For example, in my school we host new-student lunches in our conference room. Guidance staff do several "get-to-know-you" activities, answer questions, and talk about our school. I visit each meeting and stay for at least half the meeting. This allows me to make a connection with each student and to answer questions each has. If your school has a lot of students who transfer in during the year, I recommend scheduling more of these lunches. On the other hand, if transfers are low, make sure your guidance staff connects with new students for an orientation and to assist in connecting them with staff, other students, and extracurricular opportunities.

PARENT MEETINGS

As a school leader, you will have many opportunities to meet with parents. Most meetings will be positive. However, meetings for discipline issues or appeals can be challenging. This section does not delve into the complex nuances of school discipline. Instead, I'll share some strategies to diffuse challenging situations and provide examples of meetings that illustrate how to connect with parents in a positive way.

10-MINUTE OPPORTUNITIES:
POSITIVE CONTACTS

Connections are important. In our fast-paced world, many connections occur through social media. These are important, but traditional ways to connect still have plenty of value. Take ten minutes to review and reflect on my list of five ways to make positive parent connections:

Greet Parents. Parents are in and out of your main office during the school day. When you see a parent, say something like, "Hello, how are you today? How can I assist you?" Then, be an active listener. These are short, informal connections, but they send a strong message of caring and how approachable you are.

Be Visible. When the day starts and ends, greet parents at your school's designated car pickup area.

Make a Telephone Call. Most parents who get calls from school administrators expect bad news; you can change it up. Make a few positive calls each day to let parents know something special you observed their children doing.

Attend School Events. Concerts, sports, and extracurricular activities are all good opportunities to meet parents and have informal chats.

Nonwork Times. If you live in a small community, lots of people will know you. Embrace it. You cannot be the friendly person in your school but walk by people when not in school. It's important to remember that you represent your school 24/7. When you see a parent or student at the grocery store, movies, or anywhere, stop and greet them.

There will be times when what a parent wants is unreasonable; these requests can be the most challenging. On some occasions you have to say, "No, I can't do that." Then, offer a solution you think is reasonable. Unfortunately, there can be times when you cannot resolve an issue, and the parent leaves angry and/or calls the central office. If you feel a parent is going to go above you, call your central office contacts and brief them. If the situation is not manageable and you feel unsafe or threatened, firmly and politely ask the parent to leave and contact you when she or he is ready to speak appropriately. Then, call your central office contacts to brief them and seek suggestions. For all difficult meetings with parents, I recommend taking notes that detail what parents say and do; include the date, time, who attended, and your recommended course of action.

10-MINUTE TIPS: CHALLENGING SITUATIONS

Inevitably, you will encounter some angry parents through e-mails, phone calls, and office encounters. These situations can be complex, especially when you seek to understand the source of the anger. Here are some quick tips that help me:

E-Mail Quick Tip. If you receive an angry or threatening e-mail, do not write a lengthy, detailed response. E-mail the parent to set up a meeting to discuss her or his concerns—face to face or with a telephone call is usually best. If the parent e-mail has personal threats, you should contact the police. Try not to respond

(Continued)

(Continued)

outside of work hours unless you feel something is an emergency or if reaching out might help diffuse an office encounter in the morning. It's important to be aware that you are setting a precedent when you contact a parent after your day ends.

Telephone Quick Tips. There will be times when you are the recipient of parent anger during a phone call. This is never pleasant; try not to take it personally. Be a good listener, let them know you understand what they are saying, work to determine why they are angry, and seek resolution consistent with policy and practice. If you cannot resolve the problem, don't argue on the phone. Instead, set up a meeting to discuss in person.

Angry-Parent-in-the-Office Quick Tip. Be calm and escort the parent to a quiet place. It is not good in a school for adults to display anger publicly or for staff or students to see a parent being aggressive toward you. When meeting with angry people, the first thing you need to do is calm them down, speak softly, and let them know that you are here to help. Listen to their concern and work to resolve it.

10-MINUTE COLLABORATION

Take ten minutes each Monday to note when parent meetings will occur, so you do not miss the opportunity to attend. Most schools have parent groups, such as parent–teacher organizations, athletic boosters, and groups supporting the arts. Connect with these groups by attending meetings and working collaboratively with them. All schools can benefit from parent support. I have seen principals make the error of avoiding parent meetings. This is a mistake. Parents who give their time and energy to support your school should be cherished. Connect with them and support them!

10-MINUTE REFLECTIONS ON OPPORTUNITIES FOR CHANGE

What three initiatives would you choose for your school? What are some ways you focus staff and students on your initiatives?

- How can adding structure and expectations improve the effectiveness of your school?
- How will adding purpose and efficiency to the many meetings occurring in your school improve communication, culture, and learning?
- After reading this chapter, what are your top three priorities and why?

Podcast 4.1 School Initiatives

 https://resources.corwin.com/tenminute principal

5

FOSTERING CREATIVITY

You are the average of the five people you most associate with.

—Tim Ferriss

ake risks. No person ever found his or her greatness by always playing it safe. Several years ago, I spoke those very words during a faculty meeting on change. When I look back, it is clear to me that one meeting will not spark change or creativity in a school. However, one meeting can provide inspiration. Words spoken can resonate with staff and provide the foundation as well as the expectation for change.

My goal was to establish an atmosphere where staff would take risks to be creative and innovative with teaching practices. I needed to give my staff permission to be creative professionals who could benefit the students they teach. My journey had begun by repeating my core messages: encourage creativity, change, and reflect on what we do and why we do it. I continually communicated my message.

Change takes time. I wanted to give my staff permission to try new methods, to disrupt routines, and to bring more creativity into their classrooms through conversations, visuals, and article studies. To eliminate fears of my positional authority and encourage taking risks, I helped teachers understand that the goals were for everyone. We were in this together.

Creativity is part of the "Four Cs" (of the 21st century skills) teachers need to embrace to prepare students for their future. Sounds great, right? True, I never met an educator who said 21st Century Skills with a focus on creativity was a bad idea. But I have been in many schools where I simply don't see the words in action. This chapter will explore ways to bring creativity into your school and to make it the cornerstone of your leadership. I am not saying that everything needs be different. There certainly are practices that have been around for some time and are perfectly acceptable. However, creative schools look at all aspects of their offerings with the goal of exploring what can be better.

Creativity can be a force to unleash in a school, encouraging imagination and innovation to create new ideas that have value. #10MinutePrincipal

MINDSET AND CREATIVITY

Effective school leaders do not categorize students or adults. Therefore, it's important to not categorize creativity, but to accept that creativity lives in everyone. As principal, it is daunting to think I have the ability to either build a culture that honors and encourages creativity or one where creativity is extinguished. Embracing creative leadership starts with mindset.

To bring more creative thinking into a school, you and staff can start by reflecting on mindset. Through experience, I have learned that creativity cannot flourish in an overly traditional school entrenched in methodologies of the past. I have worked in schools that were proud of being traditional—schools with fixed beliefs of what was good or not good for students. Change in this type of school is challenging, but it can be done because change is a process, not an event. For schools to flourish and become more creative, for schools to unleash the creativity within each member, they need leaders, staff, and students who embrace and live a growth mindset.

Mindset matters for administrators, teachers, and all staff who work with children because mindset can have a profound impact on learning and creativity in a school. A growth mindset allows you to see potential in everyone—ourselves, other adults, and children. Fixed mindsets are harmful because they sort and select. Fixed mindsets can determine the future of students and the path of adults by developing the belief that you cannot change the trajectory of your life. Such restrictive thinking has no place in education.

A growth mindset allows us to see potential in everyone—ourselves, other adults, and children. #10MinutePrincipal

Here's an important question you need to ask: *Do I have a growth or a fixed mindset?* I believe the mindset you have influences your leadership, thinking, actions, decision-making, and who you are as a person. In her 2007 book *Mindset: The New Psychology of Success,* Carol Dweck points out the difference between a fixed and a growth mindset:

> In a fixed mindset, people believe their basic qualities, like their intelligence or talent, are simply fixed traits. They spend their time documenting their intelligence or talent instead of developing them. They also believe that talent alone creates success—without effort. They're wrong.

> In a growth mindset, people believe that their most basic abilities develop through dedication and hard work—brains and talent are just the starting point. This view creates a love of learning and resilience that is essential for great accomplishment. (pp. 8–9)

The mindset you have is a choice you can make. #10MinutePrincipal

 10-MINUTE OPPORTUNITY

Take time to consider your leadership through a ten-minute reflection. You will not find an answer in ten minutes, but if you reflect frequently in ten-minute timeframes on the questions that follow, answers will surface:

- Are you modeling and communicating a belief that learning is about time, opportunity, and effort?
- Or do you communicate through your actions and/or words that some people are simply abler than others in a world of those who can and those who cannot?
- Is there a disconnect between what you say and your actions?

10-MINUTE TIP

The reflection questions don't have yes or no answers; they require honest and sometimes uncomfortable thinking. Take ten minutes to read the reflection questions over and work toward applying them to your actions and words. Both should always be congruent. Repeat the process if you require additional time or take ten minutes to find articles staff can read to deepen their understanding of a growth mindset.

10-MINUTE COLLABORATION

Going it alone can be hard. With your administrative team, start a book study or read some articles on growth mindset. Add ten minutes once a month to a standing meeting

(Continued)

(Continued)

to discuss what you have read and share successes and challenges. Encourage staff to practice applying a growth mindset to their interactions with students and one another.

Mindset choice may appear simple, but it's not. If fully embraced, it can have a profound impact on you and those around you. The more solid, comfortable, and aware you are of your mindset, the better you will be at helping others and leading.

Often, I meet with parents who tell me they could never do math in school and that's why their child cannot succeed in math. Sometimes, the parents add that no one in their family could ever do math. This pattern can run through generations, and it is harmful because it predicts what children can and cannot do, eliminating choice. If teaching and communication by the educator or administrator reinforce a negative belief, the child will internalize that belief (Dweck, 2007). On the other hand, if the child and parents work with an educator who lives and communicates a growth mindset, an opportunity for change exists. The next time a parent or student says, "I can't do the math," you can have a different and unexpected response by using growth mindset thinking and stating, "You can't do it *yet,* but you can succeed with my support and practice." Remember, belief has the potential to shift the thinking of others, but alone it will not create change. Instead, abandoning a fixed mindset and adopting and practicing a growth mindset can enable you to provide the support needed to help students, staff, and parents work hard to successfully reach a goal or dream.

CREATIVITY AND GROWTH MINDSET: YOU CAN MAKE IT HAPPEN!

Great leaders talk about their beliefs and why they do what they do. I clearly remember the first time I watched Simon Sinek's 2009 TED talk "How Great Leaders Inspire Action." The power of the message is in its simplicity and how he teaches his message through story. Sinek reminds us that people do not necessarily care what we do or how we do it. We are drawn to people, institutions, and companies when we know why they do their work. The *WHY* tells the story. It's through story that you find inspiration, passion, and an emotional connection.

 10-MINUTE OPPORTUNITY

Watch Simon Sinek's (2009) TED Talk "How Great Leaders Inspire Action" with your school leadership team. Then, take ten minutes to do one of the following:

1. Discuss how the message is consistent with your leadership and school culture.
2. Explore what needs to change to be more focused on how you and staff are communicating why they do what they do.

 10-MINUTE TIP

Teachers, students, and parents should know through your communication why you do what you do. But action needs

(Continued)

(Continued)

to happen to allow opportunities to demonstrate how mind-set and thinking creatively can change how your work is done and how it impacts your school's culture.

Every school has a culture. If you try to collaborate with staff to create your school's culture, it most likely will be posi-tive and always evolving. Take the challenge to collaboratively develop a culture that honors creativity. However, if you, as the leader, make no effort to build your school's culture, it will still exist, but often it will not be strong and healthy. Effective schools have healthy, positive, student-centered cultures that allow for risk-taking, creativity, and positive change.

10-MINUTE COLLABORATION

Take ten minutes with your staff to discuss this question: *How can you make your school environment, your cul-ture, stronger and pinpoint your WHY?* You might have to repeat these ten-minute collaborations over several days, discussing them with different teams and/or departments. Remember, as humans we are drawn to businesses, orga-nizations, brands, and schools if we can sense excite-ment, or what is called buzz. Take another ten minutes to discuss this question: *How can you and others collaborate to create a sense of excitement that is tangible to the com-munity, parents, staff, and students?* Once you have devel-oped a creative, positive message that reflects your WHY, the good news will continue to spread among members of your school community.

COLLABORATION AND MINDSET IMPACT SCHOOL CULTURE

Richard Allen, Retired high school principal
Adjunct professor, speaker, and consultant
New Jersey

After success at my previous school, I left behind my comfort to try leading a failing school. My goal was to create a platform and develop—through collaboration, professional learning, and recognition—the growth mindset among staff and students. My hope was to create a culture that values excellence in academic and nonacademic areas.

The school was high poverty and low performing and in need of a change in culture and mindset. The superintendent had invested in the redesign of every school in the district. His belief was that environment influenced teaching and learning. However, he soon recognized that improving students' learning had more to do with instruction than new buildings My goal was to collaborate with stakeholders to change the culture from negative to positive.

My personal goal was "Excellence and No Excuses," understanding that teachers, administrators, and students would work with me to transform the building's culture. My role was simple: provide professional learning opportunities, and as teachers and administrators embraced and facilitated positive change, honor their effort and growth mindset. I listened to the stakeholders, encouraged them, and provided the training and materials needed to achieve their goals. As principal, I became a learner among learners,

(Continued)

(Continued)

always recognizing improvement and change in teaching and students' learning. My focus was on the success of others. Their successes were my successes.

Learning matters! Mindset matters! Culture matters! At the heart of school culture is the willingness of the members to embrace the vision and be willing to become ongoing learners who are excited to meet new challenges.

THINK CREATIVELY ABOUT PROFESSIONAL LEARNING

Years ago, I was speaking with a teacher about how students in the classroom would benefit from some different teaching strategies. The response was, "You never send me to conferences, so how could I do anything different?" True, we did have a tight budget, and this was before most schools had Internet access. However, this teacher was not self-motivated to improve. Instead of taking action, she waited until someone or something offered a change opportunity. Moreover, she might not have changed after attending a conference since change requires a reason followed by action. I distinguish between professional development (that implies teachers passively receive information) and professional learning (that asks teachers to be active participants).

Today, professional learning is different. Budgets in schools are still tight, but the ability to access information is much greater than it has ever been. Accessing, learning, and implementing information still resides in the decisions of the individual, but you have the ability to influence change.

Let's explore some ten-minute ideas on how to motivate staff to further their own learning. Change starts with you and can spread to those you influence. The goal is for you to collaboratively lead the change, increasing ways for staff to connect as well as take charge of their professional learning. That in turn can support an understanding of creativity and the growth mindset. When a few excited staff members get involved with social media, their excitement spreads like the common cold.

Remember, positional authority can allow a person to mandate change, but no position can mandate commitment and caring. Congruence of words and actions and how you communicate are all part of building a culture committed to improvement and creativity.

Encouraging and supporting staff to use social media for professional learning costs little but can support your staff's ongoing learning, communication, and collaboration! #10MinutePrincipal

 ## 10-MINUTE OPPORTUNITY

Here are a few questions for a ten-minute reflection:

- Are you on Twitter? If you are great! How active are you, and are you modeling how to use Twitter to grow as a professional? Are you connecting with staff and taking a lead in sharing educational content?
- If you are not on Twitter, ask yourself, why not? Give this question some honest thought. Today, it is hard

(Continued)

(Continued)

to imagine how a person could keep current in education without being on Twitter or other social media. Take ten minutes and reflect on what you can do to get more connected.

It is possible that one of your teachers is highly connected through Twitter. If so, I would recommend you connect with that person and start sharing information on teaching and learning. Connecting with staff through Twitter can inspire others to join and start sharing ideas.

 10-MINUTE TIP

Create several hashtags with teachers who use Twitter. In my school, we created a hashtag for school spirit, one for athletics, and one to celebrate our staff's creativity.

#jwmscougarblue

#jwmsathletics

#jwmsstaffinnovates

Hashtags make it easy for information to be found. My school's primary staff hashtag, #jwmsstaffinnovates, enables staff to share thoughts, ideas, and class activities all found under the hashtag, allowing anyone to find information. In addition, an effective way for staff to connect is with a Twitter List. Create a list on your Twitter page, name the list, and then invite staff from your school. A Twitter List allows all members to see tweets that have been sent.

10-MINUTE COLLABORATION

What I enjoy about Twitter is how it allows people to connect at any time. Try a Twitter chat with your staff and invite the world! Here are a few ten-minute collaborative ways to start a staff Twitter chat:

- Team up with several staff who are active on Twitter, create a hashtag, and you're on your way to starting your first Twitter chat. Promote the chat on Twitter in under ten minutes a day.
- Create a graphic to promote the tweet, a topic for the chat, questions, date, and a time. Soon, you'll be launching this growth opportunity.

My staff did a chat titled #jwmsstaffinnovates after we studied George Couros's 2015 book, *The Innovator's Mindset* (see Figure 5.1). If you'd like to read the entire conversation, go to the hashtag. What follow are some excerpts:

- ◼ "Innovative teachers think outside the box, put students first, and understand that rules, while important, don't apply if student learning is hampered by them." **#jwmsstaffinnovates**
- ◼ "Innovation is an opportunity developed with a process. Get relentless, get restless, get a process and keep your eyes on the horizon. One step every day, one change every iteration." **#jwmsstaffinnovates**
- ◼ "Having admin that not only supports but creates an atmosphere of encouragement! That's a key to why JWMS innovates!" **#jwmsstaffinnovates**

Teachers and I set a date for the chat. Two weeks before launching the chat, the school's technology resource teacher posted this image. It contains the questions to be discussed and features our school's logo and colors. To build an audience, begin tweeting about the upcoming chat about two weeks before the actual date.

I recommend you keep school Twitter chats invitational; your excitement and staff's excitement will generate interest among those who haven't joined one.

Figure 5.1   Johnson-Williams Middle School Twitter Chat Graphic

Source: Johnson-Williams Middle School (2018).

GET CREATIVE WITH GOOGLE DOCS: PROFESSIONAL ARTICLE STUDIES

When I was teaching, my principal would share professional articles and try to find time for staff to discuss them—a good idea, but impossible to schedule and coordinate during the incredibly busy school day. Lack of time during school hours was a challenge we rarely overcame, and finding time to meet and study became a yearlong frustration. Effective leaders understand the value of communication and ongoing professional learning, and today, technology has made this problem of time part of our past. Today, Google Docs can allow communication and learning to happen in a different and highly effective use of time.

Through Google Docs, teachers and administrators can engage in online conversations about professional articles. This new type of professional study can involve all members of your learning community, and you can share articles with the entire staff or target them to specific departments or groups. First, copy a favorite article and post it on Google Docs. Start the conversation by posting questions and comments, and then invite teachers to read the materials and join the discussion by writing comments. The principal and teachers can read each other's comments, continually extend the conversation, and expand their knowledge of best practices, the growth mindset, creativity, and innovation. This type of professional learning is especially effective for schools with large faculties that do not have regular full faculty meetings or common planning times for teachers. Also, Google Chats allow staff to participate whenever it's convenient, anytime of the day or evening.

Technology is part of our students' world; they are digital natives. Today, being an educator and effectively using technology go hand in hand. It is not effective to simply cheer the effort without you participating and learning with your staff. A faculty online chat shows staff a new way to communicate and to reflect on how information and their peers' responses can impact instruction. Google Docs enables you to use technology to foster collaboration, build staff's background knowledge, and transform instruction by opening communication among the entire faculty.

I do not believe technology will replace educators. I do believe all great administrators and teachers will continually develop the skills needed to use technology to transform their learning and how they approach their job. Having staff chat using Google for professional study is a game changer, an opportunity to experience transformative technology. It's also an opportunity for you to participate, communicate, and lead a new way of collaborating and learning for staff as well as bring twenty-first century learning skills into every classroom.

> **I do not believe technology will replace educators. I do believe all great administrators and teachers will continually develop the skills needed to use technology to transform their learning and how they approach their job. #10MinutePrincipal**

 ## 10-MINUTE OPPORTUNITY

Take ten minutes and find an article that speaks to all staff. Topics aligning with your school initiatives or improvement plan are great starting points. For two years, my staff made research-based grading practices a focus. Articles on grading were perfect for me to share in a Google Doc chat.

Take ten minutes and explain to staff in a meeting or through an e-mail the following: why all, including you, will be using Google to learn in a new way; the purpose of doing this particular chat; and the framework for helping the chat run smoothly. A framework includes the amount of time teachers have to read and respond and the questions to discuss.

After you launch the chat, take ten minutes each day to add comments. Give specific praise to staff when responding. Specific praise motivates students, and it does the same for adults! I recommend you explain to staff that participants use positive language when reacting to colleagues' responses. The chat is not a forum to be critical or negative.

 10-MINUTE TIP

Set a start and end date for your staff chat; I suggest you allow two weeks. When I started these, some were reluctant to try. Avoid forcing them, as this leads to compliance. Instead, take ten minutes to have conversations with those reluctant to join the chat. Show them what a chat looks like and assure them they can complete the reading/response at their convenience within the two-week window. Be positive, excited, and always participate. Remember, you set the tone.

10-MINUTE COLLABORATION

Share leadership opportunities! Invite a department chair, lead teacher, reading specialist, or school librarian to share an article and take the lead in a staff chat. Spend ten minutes with an interested staff member to discuss the article that member wants to share for a chat and how he or she plans to introduce and set guidelines for the chat.

ENCOURAGE AND CELEBRATE INNOVATIVE INSTRUCTIONAL PRACTICES

I was in my first year of being principal of Johnson-Williams Middle School and completing an observation of a revered, veteran history teacher—notes, lectures, and as I discovered in our postmeeting, tests every Friday. No different from what I experienced over thirty years ago in a high school history class I discussed on page 15. But now, as a school leader, I know our kids deserve better, much better.

John Dewey is often quoted as saying, "If we teach today's students as we taught yesterday, we rob them of tomorrow." Whether or not Dewey actually said that, those words repeatedly replay in my mind. My recent observation of a history class signaled the need for change if my school was going to meet the needs of students now and into the future. I recognized that this observation is not a picture of all history classrooms, but many middle and high school teachers use similar routines.

Change is tough. However, it's needed to develop students who can think critically and creatively, collaborate and communicate to solve problems they will surely meet in this rapidly changing world.

Sometimes in education, we do things for no real reason other than we have always done it that way. Sometimes, our thinking and personal experiences hold us back, and like Linus in the *Peanuts* cartoon, we cling to a blanket—to what's warm and familiar. Our freedom to let go of any Linus blankets we hold is critical for us to prepare students for their future. It can be tough to let go of or to change how you think. Change—anything different can be uncomfortable, but it can also be liberating. Letting go of teaching and administrative practices that are no longer relevant to twenty-first century learning needs can open doors to innovative and creative thinking.

Change—anything different can be uncomfortable, but it can also be liberating. #10MinutePrincipal

You set the tone in your school. If innovation and creative practice define your school, then, most likely, you are an innovative, creative leader who collaborates and communicates and learns with staff. The opposite is also true: If a school values and promotes lecture, students in rows, and lots of direct instruction, then as John Dewey so aptly said, that school is robbing its students of their tomorrows. We teach and prepare students for a world far different from what we experienced in school—for a future we can't always imagine and predict. Accept the leadership challenge and become a champion of innovation and creativity!

10-MINUTE OPPORTUNITY

Set priorities and address the tips your school needs most to use creativity and innovation to bring twenty-first century skills into every classroom:

- If you are new to a school, spend time the first month visiting classrooms for ten minutes at a time. Of course, you won't see all elements of teaching, but make notes on what you do see and ask questions to motivate thinking and change of practice. Here's an example of my observations and what I communicated to a teacher:

  > Teacher is engaged in a whole-class review of a test that occurred yesterday. As I observe, I see three separate groups: One group did very well on the test and does not need the review; another group seems to be benefitting from the whole-class review; and a third group had a low test grade and does not appear to get the review at all.

  > *My reflection:* I need to share some ideas on station learning with this teacher. Three stations could have been created: enrichment, guided small-group review, and final station for reteaching.

- Communicate to staff what you believe about good instruction by taking ten minutes of a meeting and ten minutes to send follow-up e-mails. Explain that you understand that taking risks to try new methods can result in failing and that's OK. The point is to reflect on a lesson and find ways to improve. Emphasize that no one will get in trouble for trying something new and missing the mark.

- Give positive feedback to staff who are trying new practices. Remember, it is always best to give short, specific praise. Ten minutes of praise each day is time well spent. A handwritten note, an e-mail, and a face-to-face conversation can give teachers short, specific feedback. Here are a few examples:

  Example 1: Last week I saw your whole-class review and shared an article with you. I am very impressed to see you trying station learning for your review today!

  Example 2: Seeing students working in pairs on a WebQuest activity speaks to you stretching as an educator. I know this is new for you, but our students need opportunities to interact with technology. Good job.

- Do a staff Google Chat on instructional strategies such as inferring, determining importance, and inquiry.
- Add *creativity* and *innovation* to every meeting agenda by providing staff with enough time to suggest items and always include schoolwide initiatives. Such collaboration encourages conversation, reflection, and showcases what you value.

10-MINUTE TIP

A staff book study is an excellent way to focus on a topic important to everybody's growth. Books on creativity in the

(Continued)

(Continued)

classroom can serve as a catalyst for change. Google is a good platform for book studies. You can use open-ended questions or a study guide the publisher often supplies; add these to Google Classroom and share with staff for responses. Negotiate with staff how many chapters they'll read for each Google Chat as well as how much time they need. All teaching staff and administrators can set aside ten minutes each day to respond to several questions from a section of the book. As with Google Chats, setting time frames is important to keep the book study moving along. Staff will appreciate knowing start and end dates.

Open-Ended Questions

- What questions did this section raise?
- What ideas and suggestions did you find useful? Explain why.
- Are there practices you can use tomorrow? How will you integrate these?
- What ideas challenge your present practices? Explain why.
- Are there ideas that you need to learn more about?
- What related articles or YouTube videos can you suggest to your colleagues?

 10-MINUTE COLLABORATION

Have a ten-minute conversation with either a grade-level team or members of a department that focuses on how they are bringing research-based creative lessons into their classrooms. I like to call these conversations "Wins and Losses." Staff need to know and feel comfortable with the idea that when trying new methods some will work and others won't. Your job in creating change is to be an encourager, a leader who communicates the value of trying new instructional practices. Be there for your staff with support and to purchase needed materials, so they can experience the positive feelings associated with teaching in new ways and watching it work for students.

SCHOOL LIBRARIES: DESIGNING CREATIVE, DYNAMIC SPACES

When I was a middle school student, our school had a very traditional library. It was a place to be silent. Vividly, I can recall several times when I was too loud and called to task by our librarian, who would yell at me from her desk. The library was a place for returning and checking out books and reading in silence. The school library was not an enjoyable place to be.

The library I describe still exists in similar variations across the country. A space that may have worked in the past no longer works for today's students. The challenge for designing a dynamic library is to use space in ways that are different from the library of my childhood experiences and possibly yours, too. I do not believe in the silent library any more than I believe in a silent classroom with perfect rows. Some parts of our past are best left in the past, and an always silent library belongs in that category. Explore the reflection questions in the 10-Minute Opportunity to help you reflect on your library and consider what changes can be made through conversations with your librarian, staff, and students immediately and over time.

Some parts of our past are best left in the past. #10MinutePrincipal

There can be times when the librarian might be resistant to change, but this is not an obstacle. By having ongoing conversations with your librarian and teachers, by sending them to schools that have outstanding libraries to gather ideas and develop a mental model of what a library can be, change will occur. It's helpful to recognize that people react to change differently: some resist, some think this too shall pass, and others embrace it. Whether change comes quickly or in smaller increments, it will have a positive impact for students and staff.

10-MINUTE OPPORTUNITY

Reflection Questions

Spend ten minutes reflecting on the questions that relate to your school's needs.

1. Does your library serve as the "family room" for your school? Or is it a place avoided by students and staff?
2. Do separate spaces exist in the library—such as a makerspace, computer centers, reading areas, and places for students to sit in comfortable furniture to collaborate?
3. Do students have opportunities to learn video technologies, such as using a green screen?

4. Has the library been analyzed for books and resources needed by students and staff?
5. How is the librarian promoting reading?
6. Is the library budget appropriate to meet the school's needs? What can be done to improve budgetary support?

To build support among staff, have ten-minute conversations at faculty meetings about questions your school should discuss. Such conversations tap into a collective vision and show staff that you value their ideas and feedback.

10-MINUTE TIP

To build a connection between you and your librarian, take ten minutes to discuss ways school libraries are changing and what one might look like in five or ten years. Next, invite your librarian to generate a list of ideas that illustrate how your library needs to change. When you have future-focused conversations, you begin to build a shared vision for your school's library, and this helps you budget present and future spending needs.

10-MINUTE COLLABORATION

As your library becomes a space used more by students and staff, an awareness of additional needs develops. Consider having your librarian do ten-minute presentations

(Continued)

(Continued)

at faculty meetings, grade-level meetings, and parent nights. These opportunities are ideal to communicate, inform, and also serve as key opportunities for you to publicly support changes for the library. In addition, consider collaborating with your librarian to podcast or use a Google extension called Screencastify to create ten-minute informational recordings of the same information shared during staff and parent meetings. Recordings can be placed on the library website, available to anyone, anytime.

CREATE STUDENT-CENTERED, FLUID CLASSROOMS

Creative use of classroom space partners well with creative, research-based teaching strategies. Of course, this is an excellent goal; however, having classroom arrangements reflect the kind of learning students do can be difficult for some to try and eventually adopt.

Images such as the classroom in Figure 5.2 can make you pause. When you look at this image, it is not much different than many of today's upper elementary or middle school classrooms in America. No computers. Rows. The teacher front and center. Could any other business or organization look as similar today as it looked half a century ago? I don't think so.

Often, teachers arrange furniture in their rooms based on classrooms they recall or rooms of teachers they admired. Set aside time to reflect on how teachers use space in their classrooms as well as whether the use of space reflects the type of instruction

Figure 5.2   **Traditional, Teacher-Centered Class**

iStock.com/shaunl

students experience. Remember, sitting in groups but doing the same work completed in rows is not effective change. Space can and should be flexible and adjust for instruction and collaboration.

> **Remember, sitting in groups but doing the same work completed in rows is not effective change. #10MinutePrincipal**

A couple of years ago I was working on our school budget and sought input from staff on furniture needs. I was confident staff would request tables for their classrooms instead of desks. Why such confidence? At meetings, I had been communicating the need to shift to new furniture to allow for flexible grouping and movement in the classroom. This conversation was always in tandem with new instructional initiatives and the need to create collaborative opportunities for students. To my surprise, two teachers said they wanted desks like Ginny, who had perfect rows and refused to change. What I needed to do was spend more time communicating my message. Looking back, I wish I had taken more time to discuss these changes with teachers because in this case my attempt to build consensus was unsuccessful; I made a top-down decision and said no to desks. I should have reflected on whether teachers were receiving and accepting my message and continued to discuss issues with them and show visuals of diverse room arrangements until we reached consensus.

10-MINUTE OPPORTUNITY

There are many ways to communicate a message, but it only works if the message is heard. I encourage you to use three ways of sharing information as you schedule ten-minute opportunities:

- Hold repeated conversations.
- Show visuals that clearly illustrate your intentions.
- Read and discuss articles with Google Docs or through small-group discussions.

Creative and innovative leaders make mistakes, but they learn from them and choose improved communication and collaborations with staff over blaming others or making an autocratic decision. My failure to seek feedback from staff about desks can be a win for you. My message failed to resonate with all staff because I relied only on verbal communication; I omitted studying articles through Google Docs and using visual opportunities for impact and clearer understanding. When you communicate, think of multiple ways to create buy-in with people.

10-MINUTE TIP

Take ten minutes to discuss Internet sites that show fluid class arrangements and invite teachers to revisit these. Share the blog post "On Flexible Seating" (2017) by Pernille Ripp, an outstanding seventh-grade teacher, who discusses her move from traditional to fluid class arrangements. Take ten minutes to discuss this blog post at faculty, team, or department meetings. Set aside another ten minutes to find articles you can post on Google Docs. You can also invite teachers to find articles; those who are enthusiastic about change will help you.

10-MINUTE COLLABORATION

Encourage staff to observe colleagues' classrooms for ten minutes to see how some use space in nontraditional ways, reflecting the diverse learning experiences of students. In addition, take ten minutes to e-mail staff some reflective questions like the three that follow:

1. How is this class seating arrangement different from more traditional classrooms?

(Continued)

(Continued)

2. Did the instructional model work with the seating or against it? Explain why.

3. What are a few changes you could make to your room? Explain why you selected these.

Invite teachers to discuss the questions at team and/or department meetings. Then, schedule ten-minute meetings with small groups to learn where teachers are in the process.

The artist Pablo Picasso said, "Others have seen what is and asked why. I have seen what could be and asked why not." His statement reflects a mindset I'm hoping you will adopt. Your mindset determines much about who you are and what you stand for. To bring creativity into your school, give yourself and your staff permission to be creative. Don't just communicate a belief in creativity; apply what you ask of others to yourself. Creativity and mindset are not things we switch on and off. I have told my staff many times you cannot be a creative person at work and the opposite at home. Nor can you communicate and live a growth mindset for part of your life and not have it exist in other parts.

This chapter began with a simple quote by Tim Ferriss (Robinson, 2017): "You are the average of the five people you most associate with." The truth in this statement invites you and me to consider the people we spend time with and ask whether it enhances creative thinking and growth mindset or if it does the opposite.

10-MINUTE REFLECTIONS
ON OPPORTUNITIES FOR CHANGE

Consider your personal creativity and how you encourage, enhance, and inspire others by thinking about these questions:

- Are you modeling, communicating, and living a mindset to encourage growth, innovation, and creativity?
- What ten-minute tips will you use to guide your journey?
- After reading this chapter and reflecting on your school, what is affirmed and what needs to change?
- When staff try new ways to do what they do, how do you know if it's working?

Podcast 5.1 Mindset Matters

https://resources.corwin.com/tenminute principal

6

CHOOSE
YOUR PATH

Ophelia: We know what we are, but not what we may be.
—William Shakespeare, *Hamlet,* Act IV, Scene 5

Have you ever had days where you feel as if nothing's been accomplished? Each summer during my first few years as principal, I would feel overwhelmed by the job, pondering my next steps. I had so many ideas and felt unsure about where to start.

One summer day, I watched a movie called *City Slickers* (Smith, 1991), starring Billy Crystal, Jack Palance, and Daniel Stern. In the movie, three friends vacation on a two-week cattle drive from New Mexico to Colorado, each searching for meaning in his life. They have many adventures along the way, and they learn some wisdom from a seasoned cattle hand named Curly (Palance). He explains his secret of life: "Discover your one purpose." When the movie ended, I had a lightbulb moment. My one purpose would always be to champion, to advocate for students by putting their needs first. Finding your one purpose allows you to focus on what's important in your job. Having a focus can diminish overwhelming feelings about where to start. You begin by making decisions that are best for students, and at times, this will lead to meaningful change.

When you propose new changes, staff's reactions can range from negative to positive. Sometimes, when you lead you start out alone with a good or great idea that others are apprehensive about. Sometimes, you need to take people to a place they have not thought of or may fear. You can minimize the challenges by building consensus. However, don't presume you can get one hundred percent on board. Administrators who seek complete approval of ideas or initiatives don't get much done. The most important message I can share with you is to start. Part of leadership is creating a sense of purpose and moving forward to reach new goals. Unite students, staff, and a community behind a sense of purpose that generates passion and helps people find inspiration for their work. Model your mindset, model risk-taking, and model a positive outlook! Work with staff to prioritize areas for change as you and your team move forward.

MOVING FORWARD

When you build commitment toward a well-articulated vision and common goals, your odds of achieving success escalate. You will face choices that define your leadership. Make sure your choices are consistent with your core values and the values of your school. Your choices have the ability to draw people to you, away from you, or cause people to fear you. This is a big responsibility, one of many that come with any leadership position.

Would people with whom you work agree you are a person of integrity and are consistently trustworthy? At the core of this question is doing what you say you will do again and again. Such consistency helps you build trust and organizational commitment. Without trust and relationships, you cannot lead. As an educator, if you believe in putting students first, and I hope you do, ask yourself this question: *Do my actions support this belief or create contradictions?* Are you making daily decisions that align with a shared vision and goals or in opposition to these? Continually reflect on the connection between your words and actions; fine-tune them so they align and pulse the messages and beliefs you want to communicate.

Beware the lure of positional authority; making people do things does not build commitment. Such actions can be defined as autocratic, compliance-based leadership. Most people need a job, and some will allow themselves to be treated poorly just because they need the job. This type of "leading" will never build a staff committed to a vision and goals. Yes, it makes people "do" things, but it cannot make people care. Great leaders inspire others!

FIND YOUR PATH

Know your purpose and travel pathways that help you reach it. I can recall times when I spent too much time reacting to problems. Problems will always arise, but if you keep your purpose in mind as you handle them, you can move your staff to a collective vision and collective decisions.

As you move forward with your career, work to inspire others, to make a difference for students and staff. Always strive to build commitment focused on the pillars of leadership and your personal *why*. People who support each other, care for each other, and commit to a common vision are better team members and develop their leadership capacities. Be the leader you hope to be.

NEW TO ADMINISTRATION

During your first year, pay particular attention to trust and relationships because both are foundational to being an effective leader. Through relationship building, you'll come to know members of your school's community, as well as their values and beliefs. Take some time to review the pillars of leadership from Chapter 1. Each pillar relies on the others; together, they form a foundation for success.

With trusting relationships and an understanding of culture in place, you can collaborate with staff to develop a vision for your school. Slowly, gradually, and collectively decide on one to three schoolwide initiatives to tackle during your second year. Communicate the vision and initiatives to all stakeholders through collaborative conversations, videos, and podcasts. Educate them and find ways to include them in the process. Finally, always recognize hard work by sending an e-mail and/or writing a personal note. Reserving time to show people that you recognize their commitment, work ethic, professional learning, and dedication to their students sends the message that you care and value their contributions.

When you show by words and actions that success results from collaboration, your staff will support their school's journey toward excellence. Moreover, you strengthen the bonds between you and all community members, as well as the bonds among themselves. When leaders cultivate strong, trusting bonds and relationships, they can inspire others to work for changes that transform a school's vision into reality.

EXPERIENCED ADMINISTRATORS

Revisit the chapters of this book and create a short list of several areas to start your journey of change. Don't write a huge list. Be selective and start with a few ideas you can initiate by collaborating with staff. Initiative frenzy, or change for the sake of trying new ideas, causes anxiety and frustration among teachers because they never spend enough time on an initiative to see if it's supporting students. Soon, you will feel overwhelmed, and when assessing change, you'll find that nothing has taken root. Start small. Identify and go for some wins. Then, build on the momentum.

GIVE YOURSELF THE GIFT OF TIME

It will take time to become the leader you want to be. Therefore, be patient and be a learner. Give hope to and have faith in students and staff. Choose to make a difference and be kind. Take risks. Great educators never play it safe all the time. Believe in students, and remember that the ones who stress you out are probably the students who need you the most. When you think things are not working or you're not connecting with students or staff, keep in mind that you never know when you make a difference.

Make the choice every day to be a positive and compassionate person. Avoid negativity. Negative educators create negative environments and often bring out the worst in students' behavior. It's challenging for students to learn in a negative environment, and staff will never flourish when surrounded by negativity. When you work with staff, support them. Hire new teachers who exude empathy, kindness, and a love for teaching and learning. Be patient. Change takes time. Take care of yourself because leadership roles are taxing—find something that's just for you, such as going to the gym to work out, taking relaxing walks, reading mysteries, and the like.

Set aside time to give to yourself, too. Remember, if you can rally and unite students, staff, and the community around a strong purpose—a collective vision—magic can and will happen!

Audere est facere—**To dare is to do. #10MinutePrincipal**

Podcast 6.1 Your Path

 https://resources.corwin.com/tenminute principal

REFERENCES

Couros, G. (2015). *The innovator's mindset: Empower learning, unleash talent, and lead a culture of creativity.* San Diego, CA: Dave Burgess Consulting.

de Saint-Exupéry, A. (1959). *Citadelle.* Paris, France: Gallimard. Retrieved from https://quoteinvestigator.com/category/antoine-de-saint-exupery/

Dweck, C. (2007). *Mindset: The new psychology of success.* New York, NY: Ballantine Books.

Frey, N., & Fisher, D. (2011). *The formative assessment action plan: Practical steps to more successful teaching and learning.* Alexandria, VA: Association for Supervision and Curriculum Development.

Fullan, M. (2010). *The awesome power of the principal.* Retrieved from https://www.naesp.org/sites/default/files/resources/2/Principal/2010/MarchApril/M-Ap10.pdf

Hattie, J. (2016, July 11). Third Annual Visible Learning Conference: Mindframes and Maximizers, Washington, DC.

Kemp, C. (2018). 25 school leaders to follow on Twitter. Retrieved from http://mrkempnz.com/2018/05/25-school-leaders-to-follow-on-twitter.html

Kouzes, J. M., & Posner, B. Z. (2006). *The leadership challenge* (3rd ed.). Hoboken, NJ: John Wiley & Sons.

Peterson, J. C., & Kaplan, D. A. (2016). *The 10 laws of trust: Building the bonds that make a business great.* New York, NY: AMACOM.

Ripp, P. (2017). On flexible seating [Blog post]. Retrieved from https://pernillesripp.com/2017/12/28/on-flexible-seating/

Robinson, M. (2017, Jan. 11). Tim Ferriss: 'You are the average of the five people you most associate with.' *Business Insider.* Retrieved from https://www.businessinsider.com/tim-ferriss-average-of-five-people-2017–1

Sergiovanni, T. J. (1992). *Moral leadership: Getting to the heart of school leadership.* San Francisco, CA: Jossey-Bass.

Sheninger, E., & Rubin, T. (2017). *BrandED: Tell your story, build relationships, and empower learning.* San Francisco, CA: Jossey-Bass.

Sinek, S. (2009). *How great leaders inspire action* [Video file]. Retrieved from https://www.ted.com/talks/simon_sinek_how_great_leaders_inspire_action?language=en&utm_campaign=tedspread&utm_medium=referral&utm_source=tedcomshare

Smith, I. (Producer). (1991). *City slickers* [Motion picture]. Los Angeles, CA: Castle Rock Entertainment.

Starbucks. (n.d.). Retrieved October 27, 2008, from http://www.starbucks.com/aboutus

INDEX

Note: Page numbers in *italics* refer to figures.

A SAGE Publishing Company

Helping educators make the greatest impact

CORWIN HAS ONE MISSION: to enhance education through intentional professional learning.

We build long-term relationships with our authors, educators, clients, and associations who partner with us to develop and continuously improve the best evidence-based practices that establish and support lifelong learning.